FRANCES LYNCH

MEGALITHIC TOMBS AND LONG BARROWS IN BRITAIN

SHIRE ARCHAEOLOGY

Cover photograph
Pentre Ifan, Pembrokeshire: a portal dolmen with façade.

British Library Cataloguing in Publication Data
Lynch, Frances, 1938-
Megalithic tombs and long barrows in Britain.
– (Shire archaeology; 73)
1. Megalithic monuments – Great Britain
2. Great Britain – Antiquities
I. Title
936.1'01
ISBN 0 7478 0341 2

Published by
SHIRE PUBLICATIONS LTD
Cromwell House, Church Street, Princes Risborough,
Buckinghamshire HP27 9AA, UK.

Series Editor: James Dyer.

ISBN 0 7478 0341 2.

First published 1997.

Printed in Great Britain by
CIT Printing Services, Press Buildings,
Merlins Bridge, Haverfordwest, Pembrokeshire SA61 1XF.

Contents

Acknowledgements

In writing a book like this one's debt to other workers in the field is obvious: I have borrowed their facts, their ideas and their illustrations shamelessly and on a scale too wide to acknowledge everybody. But I should like to record my particular debt to my original tutor, the late T. G. E. Powell, and to my fellow authors of *Megalithic Enquiries in the West of Britain*, Jack Scott and the late John Corcoran. I am also most grateful to Audrey Henshall for her encouragement of a very raw postgraduate, to Paul Ashbee and to Ian Kinnes, from whose books I have quarried deeply.

I am especially grateful to the Series Editor, James Dyer, for his invitation to write this book and for all his help during its production, not least his generous loan of photographs. I should also like to thank Graham Ritchie for his help with the Scottish photographs; Aubrey Burl, who has very kindly allowed his collection to be used; and Alistair Whittle and Ian Hodder for the loan of excavation photographs. I am also grateful to the late Professor Stuart Piggott, Paul Ashbee, Colin Renfrew and Blaise Vyner for permission to reproduce drawings from their publications. Finally I should like to thank all the staff of Shire Publications for their care and forbearance.

Frances Lynch

University of Wales, Bangor

4

List of illustrations

1
Introduction: background to monumentality

The stone tombs of the first farming communities in Europe can still inspire awe, wonder and curiosity even in modern populations familiar with Gothic cathedrals and towering skyscrapers. These seemingly precarious blocks of stone have survived through a changing landscape for more than six thousand years, the oldest built structures in Europe. Alongside these stone monuments we should not forget the contemporary wooden ones, equally monumental in their day, but now reduced to low ploughed mounds and invisible postholes.

These structures belong to the first 'interventionist' economy in Europe, when hunting and gathering were gradually replaced by the growing of food and the control of useful animal populations. This change in fundamental lifestyle emerged in the Near East, where suitable crops grew wild, and was spread across Europe along the valley of the Danube and the shores of the Mediterranean through pressure to find fertile virgin land as much as through the competitive success of the system.

The change from a hunting economy, however sophisticated, to a system which demands foresight and positive action is one which is likely to have induced feelings of responsibility and anxiety in its practitioners, always having to look ahead to the next year's harvest and the continuing fertility of their herds. It is this change of attitude which is thought to lie behind the apparently sudden concern with the burial of the dead and the fostering of the memory of ancestors.

However, the farmers of the Danube valley, the most thorough-going of the new interventionists, did not build elaborate or monumental tombs. The dead were buried very simply in small graves close to the settlements. The monumental tombs belong to the regions which fringe this primary focus of European farming. Large stone tombs are to be found in southern Spain and Portugal, in south-western France and in Brittany, where they are exceptionally impressive, varied and interesting. In Britain and Ireland stone monuments are to be found in most western areas, and in the south and east their equivalents were built in wood. There are many stone tombs in south Sweden and Denmark, and in Holland and north Germany boulders were used where available. Elsewhere, notably in Poland, wood was preferred.

These tombs, which vary in detail of design and ritual, all share the element of monumentality and, where the evidence is available, we know that they were used collectively. Their size alone demonstrates

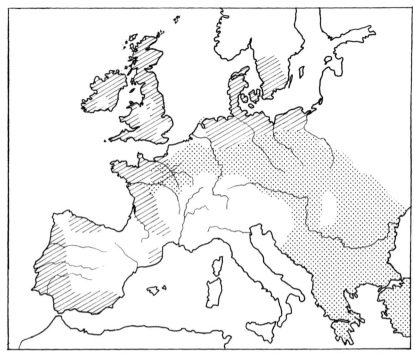

1. European distribution of monumental tombs (hatched) and Danubian and related farming cultures (stippled). Mediterranean basin cultures are not shown.

that they are the product of co-operative action and must represent an important investment of time and resources for people who would have been living at little more than subsistence level. Their distribution suggests that they belong to communities at the edge of the new economy, in areas perhaps where two populations, new farmers and indigenous hunters, may have been forced to live together. We will never know the full story, but the peculiar distribution of these huge tombs suggests that the impact of new ideas had an especially pronounced effect in this contact zone.

One of the astonishing things is that this effect should have been so similar over so large and diverse a territory. This used to be explained as the effect of a unifying religion passed along the Atlantic Façade but more recently regional diversity has been stressed, each province reacting in a slightly different way to the pressures of the new life.

It is believed that in most areas the earliest communal tombs were quite small and that they might be simple stone or wooden boxes (cists) only subsequently covered with a single mound to initiate the tradition of collectivity and monumentality which is the hallmark of the later series. Such a sequence, culminating in the great pyramids, can be historically demonstrated in Egypt. Several regions might claim to be primary areas for such developments, for radiocarbon dates do not show any single geographical area as the source.

However, Brittany and western France can claim both early and influential developments, perhaps because mesolithic burials there are rather commoner and more elaborate than elsewhere. By the mid fifth millennium BC in southern Brittany there are burials grouped under very long mounds; by the beginning of the fourth millennium BC passage graves, often incorporating shattered pieces of earlier monuments, have appeared and later centuries show local variations and elaborations of this style. The appearance of passage graves may involve the adoption of ideas shared by other groups in different parts of Europe. Certainly during the middle neolithic (4000-3500 cal BC), as populations expand and the landscape fills up, it is possible to recognise several instances of borrowed ideas of design and ritual custom, both between regions within mainland Europe and between Europe and Britain. In the late neolithic (3500-2900 cal BC) a particular type of long mound is common to all of northern France and Germany, but by this stage in southern Britain the tradition of collective and monumental burial, which had begun around 4000 cal BC, was coming to an end.

2
History of research

Large stone monuments have been the subject of curiosity at all periods but their serious study dates only from the sixteenth and seventeenth centuries AD, when many were first robbed of their covering mounds by agricultural activities.

In the nineteenth century the passion for classification and organisation led to several major surveys, such as Fergusson's *Rude Stone Monuments in All Countries* (1872), and much fundamental debate. It was established that the structures were tombs and not 'druidical altars' and were originally covered by cairns or earthen mounds.

The contemporary diffusionist ethos led to the view that the widespread occurrence of these 'megalithic' tombs might represent a single religious impulse emanating from one source, likely to be the eastern Mediterranean, whence so many civilising movements had come. This source was variously identified as Egypt or Crete, where pyramids or *tholoi* could provide models. In the absence of any independent dating for the western European tombs, such a view, which postulated a spread of 'megalithic missionaries' through the Mediterranean to Spain and northwards to Brittany, Britain and Scandinavia, was geographically

2. Nineteenth-century view of Bryn Celli Ddu, Anglesey, showing the remains of a mound covering the capstone.

plausible and was sustained into the twentieth century by such notable thinkers as V. G. Childe.

In the first half of the twentieth century more detailed fieldwork in various parts of Europe provided a greater understanding of the variety of designs of stone chambers and excavation exposed the remains of wooden ones. This work led to the recognition of various broad strands within the 'megalithic religion', notably the distinction between *passage graves* (where the chamber and entrance passage are differentiated) and *gallery graves* (in which the burial chamber is of uniform width) and between *long barrows* (earth mounds with wooden chambers) and *long cairns* (stone mounds). G. E. Daniel's *The Megalith Builders of Western Europe* (1958) was a landmark in these studies. The former distinction has been played down in more recent writing because the 'gallery graves' have been divided into independent regional groups, but it should be admitted that the concept of a 'family' of passage graves may still have some life in it, for real similarities over a wide area remain open to interpretation as evidence for implantation of a developed idea. The builders' choice of wooden or stone chambers is born of necessity and leads inevitably to some different practices, but at the philosophical level it is increasingly recognised that all monumental tombs share the same impulses and concerns.

Since the 1960s scholars have tended to concentrate less on the broad similarities across Europe and more on regional groups where a locally coherent story might be reconstructed. This trend has been reinforced by the development of radiocarbon dating, which has demolished the simple primacy of the eastern Mediterranean and Iberia and shown the phenomenon of monumental burial to be developing in many parts of Europe at about the same time and springing from essentially local reactions to new economies and ways of thinking.

During the 1930s great efforts were made to provide a framework of relative dating by establishing schemes of typological development. Arguments taken from biology and architectural history were used to show a line of development from one tomb design to another. The discussion of the sequence amongst Cotswold-Severn cairns – from terminal transepted chambers, to lateral chambers in cairns with false portals, to cairns with no portal but only a blind forecourt – is a good instance (figures 36 and 40). Unfortunately the lack of established starting points within these arguments means that they can often be reversed with equal logic.

One aspect of typological discussion which has been more generally useful is the recognition, since the excavation in the 1960s of such sites as Dyffryn Ardudwy in Merioneth (figure 28), that many tombs are the product of several distinct periods of building. This has enabled many

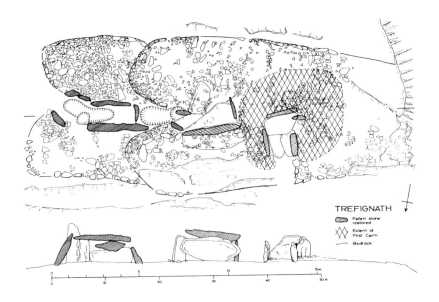

3. Trefignath, Anglesey, a multi-chambered cairn developed over three periods. (Plan and section from Lynch, 1991.)

elements of complex sites to be disentangled and placed in firm stratigraphic sequences (figure 3). Consequently it is possible to recognise the individual components of new ideas and to measure their impact in new areas. The recognition of demonstrable and potential multi-period sites has resolved many of the problems associated with local groups of box-like stone chambers, as the work of Jack Scott, John Corcoran and Audrey Henshall in Scotland has shown.

Alongside this detailed typological analysis, recent megalithic studies have turned to consider more intangible questions relating to the role of tombs and monumentality in neolithic society. Attention has been directed to the peripheral distribution of the tombs in Europe and the reasons why this phenomenon should arise where farming impacted on confident populations of mesolithic hunters. The relative timescales of burial use and subsequent maintenance have also raised questions about the social significance of the tombs, over and above their use as containers of bones.

3
Systems of burial

Although we realise now that neolithic tombs must have had broad religious and social roles, more akin to those of a church than just a family vault, it is the evidence for their burial role which is clearest.

This evidence is derived mainly from the southern English wooden chambers, where, hidden beneath long earthen mounds, the contents have been protected from later disturbance. Bone very seldom survives in the stone chambers of the west and north because of both later human curiosity and the acidity of the soils. Moreover the frequent use of cremation in the west makes interpretation more difficult.

The surviving evidence normally indicates collective burial of men, women and children. Their bones are physically mixed and it is seldom possible to recognise any particular individual, either as a discrete group of bones or by any accompanying personal possessions (figure 4). This evidence suggests that the mass of bone is important, not as a series of individuals, but as a group of anonymous ancestors amongst whom any distinctions of wealth or status have been obliterated. This situation contrasts strongly with that of the succeeding bronze age, when individual burials with personal possessions may be interpreted as evidence for a ranked society headed by chieftains who wielded sole power. This is not to say that power was not exercised in the neolithic – the very

4. Skendleby, Lincolnshire: the bone deposit comprising eight individuals intermixed. (After Phillips, 1936.)

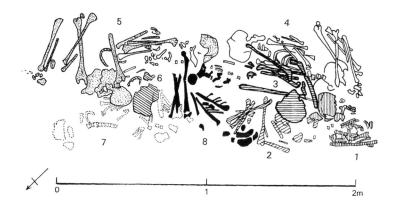

0   1   2m

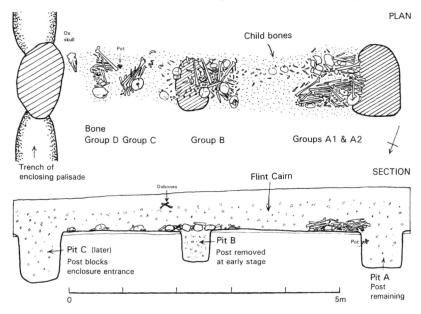

5. Plan and section of the bone deposit, Fussell's Lodge, Wiltshire (see also figure 16). (After Ashbee, 1966.)

monumentality of the graves suggests powerful control – but that power (perhaps better labelled 'authority' in this period) was likely to have resided not in an individual but in a group – an oligarchy or perhaps theocracy – legitimised through their relationship to a group of ancestors, individually anonymous but collectively powerful as mediators between the gods and their own descendants.

This group of ancestors includes men, women and children but the overall numbers and the occasional imbalance between the sexes and age groups suggests that they are not a true sample of the population, but a selected group. Unfortunately we cannot guess at the selection criteria used, especially as the absence of formal grave goods removes the possibility of identifying their occupation or status in life.

Burial deposits have survived intact from several monuments in southern England, where a fairly standard pattern may be recognised in both stone and wooden chambers.

The bones at Wayland's Smithy, Oxfordshire, a small long barrow with a wooden chamber, lay on a stone paving within a narrow burial zone defined by two large posts. At the far end was a single crouched body and other bodies had been laid forward of it but those in the centre had been disturbed and covered by a heap of bone representing at least

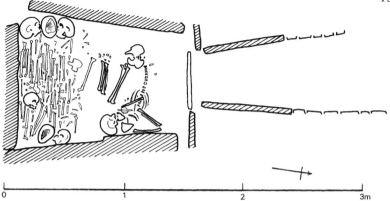

6. Plan of bones in the north chamber, Lanhill, Wiltshire, a Cotswold-Severn cairn. (After Keiller and Piggott, 1938.)

fourteen individuals deposited when already partially decayed: some joints were in articulation, most were not. Four layers could be recognised in this heap, perhaps indicating that bodies had been added on four separate occasions.

At Fussell's Lodge, Wiltshire, the bones may have been brought into the tomb as dry bones, in square boxes which were then laid on the floor (figure 5). The inner box held the incomplete remains of thirteen adults and four children. Not only were small bones missing, but also long bones and skulls. The central group represents eleven adults and eleven children, their bones very fragmentary and weathered. The two outermost groups of bones look like intact, undisturbed skeletons, but each consists of two incomplete adults.

At Lanhill, a Cotswold-Severn cairn in Wiltshire where the north chamber was totally undisturbed, an adult lay across the chamber with the bones of several others tidied to the back (figure 6). In one case a skull and lower jaw from different individuals had been carefully, but incorrectly, reassembled. Facial characteristics suggested a family relationship between several of the dead in this chamber.

Many explanations have been adduced for the condition of the bones in these tombs. At the beginning of the twentieth century it was often thought that the remains might be those of a chieftain and followers sacrificed on his death. This view was never really tenable because few chambers could have held so many fresh bodies and it is now firmly rejected because there is no evidence for such a social structure. The evidence from Lanhill suggests that shortly after death a body might be brought to the burial chamber and there left to decay, undisturbed until the space was required for another person, when the original body would be swept to the back, a process which might be repeated several times. The four articulated skeletons at Nutbane, Hampshire, must also represent bodies which had not been moved since death.

However, the frequent discovery of disarticulated and incomplete skeletons with visibly weathered bones suggests that the rituals of death and burial were usually more complicated than at Lanhill or Nutbane, involving a period of exposure or perhaps temporary burial before final deposition within the tomb. The location of exposure sites has been a matter of debate. Human bones have been found in the ditches of causewayed enclosures (contemporary hilltop sites used for public gatherings) and the recent excavation of one at Hambledon Hill in Dorset provides good evidence for the exposure there of partial corpses. Some have suggested that mortuary enclosures, which have structural parallels to long barrows but lack bones and a covering mound, might have been used for this purpose. Others have suggested that the postholes immediately in front of many long barrows might have held the posts of an exposure tower or platform. However, convincing evidence of this, perhaps the discovery there of the small bones so often missing from skeletons in the tombs, was not found until 1996. The discovery then of just such a scatter of small bones at Stoney Middleton in Derbyshire promises to throw more light on this elusive stage.

Though most authorities now agree that the process of burial was a two-stage affair, there are still a number of uncertainties. For instance, we do not know whether there was one final act of collective burial or whether exposed bones were brought in on several occasions. Nor do we know whether or not earlier bones might have been completely cleared out of some chambers.

The situation in the stone chambers seems broadly similar but in the west and north cremation is common. The mass of cremated bone found by early excavators in the passage graves of northern Scotland indicates a collective ritual but defies detailed analysis. In several instances this layer was overlaid by unburnt bones.

In Wales and south-west Scotland little evidence survives, but the existence of formally closed chambers raises the question of whether they could ever have been used successively and whether they might have contained only one body. Other small monuments of possibly early neolithic date, such as the 'rotunda' at Notgrove, Gloucestershire, and the burial at Radley, Oxfordshire, may belong to a short-lived phase of single burial which might be compared to the grouped cists under the Breton long mounds. Such atypical monuments continually remind us that no generalisation concerning prehistoric life can ever be secure, but the bulk of our surviving evidence suggests that collectivity became and remained the norm until the late neolithic.

The incomplete nature of the skeletons has already been mentioned

7. Skulls in the side chamber, Isbister, Orkney. (Photograph John Hedges.)

and is ascribed to loss in transfer to the grave. However, this cannot be the sole explanation, for many large bones, skulls and long bones are missing. Taken together with the discovery of human bone at causewayed enclosures, this has been interpreted as evidence for the use of tombs as storehouses for ritual material from which ancestral bones might be taken for ceremonies among the living. The sorting of bones, especially the striking instance at Isbister in the Orkneys where all the skulls were gathered together into one small chamber (figure 7), might be taken as further evidence for this extra role – one which might explain continued interest in the tombs long after active burial had ceased.

The concept of grave goods, equipment to accompany the individual into the other world, seems to be alien to the anonymous collectivism of British neolithic society. Very few artefacts are found in tombs of this date, only the occasional flint or bone tool and sherds of broken pottery, together with some animal bones. These finds are normally interpreted as the remains of funeral ceremonies and feasts.

There is some regional variation in these customs but nowhere are overtly religious symbols placed in the tombs, as they are in Iberia. In the south and in Wales the finds are especially sparse and pottery is deposited, often in front of the tombs, as broken sherds. In Scotland much more pottery is placed with the bones in the chambers and often as complete pots. There is little difference in Britain between passage graves and other types of tomb in respect of grave goods.

4

Analysis of burial structures

Despite variation of materials and regional preferences in design certain recurrent elements can be recognised in the structure of monumental tombs across Britain. Three elements – the burial space or chamber, some emphasis on the entrance (or apparent entrance), and a covering mound of earth or stone – are virtually universal. However, the mound may be added at a much later date and may develop an independent significance, for monuments which cover no burials – essentially cenotaphs – have been recognised.

The burial space is normally at the east end of the monument, a narrow rectangle, always small in relation to the final covering mound. This space may be open or closed: often open in wooden monuments, and normally assumed to be enclosed and roofed in stone ones. Open spaces may be defined by pits or large postholes at either end. Evidence from Fussell's Lodge (figure 5) and Nutbane shows that the space could be extended during the period of burial use by removing a post. The questions of definition by pit or by standing post, and the height of the posts, are matters of interpretation of often difficult field evidence.

In northern England excavation suggests that the sides of the 'chamber' were defined by low banks and the structure might have been roofed by timbers lying on them; at Haddenham in Cambridgeshire the chamber, preserved by waterlogging, had a floor, sides and roof of large planks (figure 8). However, at Nutbane and probably at Fussell's Lodge the bodies and bones lying between the posts simply had a light covering of branches or stones.

Greater variation can be recognised amongst stone chambers because details can be studied even at unexcavated sites. However, the essence of most designs is the rectangular box and it is becoming clear that tombs such as the Clyde group and the portal dolmens (see chapter 7) are not so very different in concept from closed wooden chambers like that at Haddenham. This is especially true of the putatively early stage when stone chambers had fixed closing slabs (figure 9). In portal dolmens this front is very impressive but the burial space remains a simple box-like structure. In Clyde tombs the vertical emphasis is never so strong but the burial space is extended by multiplication of box-like chambers. The evidence from Haddenham and the sequence of pits or posts at other sites suggests that this trend may exist at wooden sites, though specialisation in the use of these compartments cannot be systematically demonstrated.

The design of the passage grave, which interposes a passage of vary-

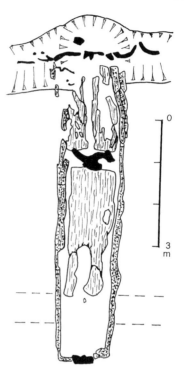
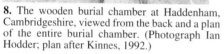

8. The wooden burial chamber at Haddenham, Cambridgeshire, viewed from the back and a plan of the entire burial chamber. (Photograph Ian Hodder; plan after Kinnes, 1992.)

9. The chamber at Cairnholy I, Kirkcudbrightshire, from the back. Note the resemblance of the back chamber to Street House and Haddenham (see plan, figure 22). (Photograph James Dyer.)

ing length between the burial space and the outside world, seems to belong to a very different tradition (figure 31). The burial chamber is normally round or polygonal rather than rectangular and is both wider and higher than the passage. The entrance to the passage is low and architecturally understated, another contrast with the box chambers, whose entrance features become increasingly important.

Entrance features take a number of forms, all suggesting a point of focus between the worlds of the living and the dead. It is interesting, however, that it is seldom possible to pass between these worlds at this point because the apparent entrance is rarely easily accessible. In most wooden monuments and many stone ones the actual doorway is blocked. In portal dolmens it can be shown that this blocking is part of the original construction (figure 28); the unusual preservation at Haddenham revealed that there, too, access could have been obtained only by lifting the roof.

This would suggest that activities in front of the tomb did not demand regular access to the burial space. The exact nature of these activities can only be guessed; the remains of fires and the apparently deliberate spreading of occupation debris are clues which are difficult to interpret.

The simplest method of emphasising the point of focus is by giving it extra height. Deep postholes suggest high posts at many wooden chambers though at Haddenham the surviving timbers suggest a structure little more than 1 metre high. In portal dolmens the impressive 'doorway' is their defining characteristic (figure 29). At Clyde tombs the provision of separate portal stones and their increasing height are part of a trend towards greater emphasis which eventually encompasses wide forecourts backed by high façades (figures 22 and 23).

A façade of tall posts to either side of the 'entrance' is regularly revealed by excavation at earth and wood monuments. It is less common at stone monuments, which suggests that it is a borrowed idea, adding theatricality to the setting of ceremonies. In the south of England wooden façades are normally straight and may form part of an enclosing palisade which defines the area later to be covered by the mound (figure 16). In the north the façades are more often concave in plan, with projecting horns which define a wide ceremonial stage or forecourt (figure 18). It is this semicircular design which is echoed in the stone façades which occur in south-west Scotland and more regularly in the north of Ireland. Since the simplest stone tombs, which are believed to be the earliest, lack these façades it may be argued that the idea was introduced from the east.

In the south of England the straight façade may often be fronted by an array of postholes, often interpreted as evidence for a tower or 'forebuilding'. The form that these structures took is variable and it is difficult to judge whether such arrangements of posts represent roofed porches, exposure towers on which bodies might have been laid or

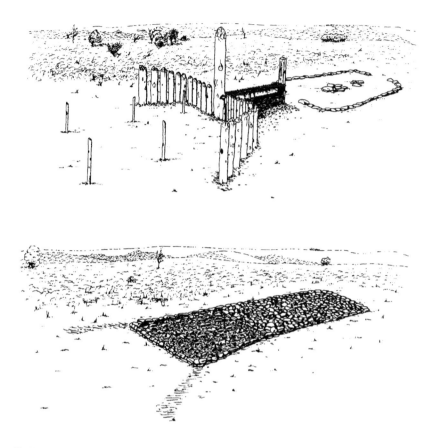

10. Reconstruction of the burial chamber (top) and subsequent covering mound at Street House, North Yorkshire. (Drawing by Louise Hutchinson from Vyner, 1984.)

simply more confined forecourts. It is perhaps relevant that the Cotswold-Severn cairns often have narrow, funnel-shaped forecourts which may echo these wooden counterparts. The shape suggests that ceremonies in that region may have been less public, restricted to a smaller congregation.

As already mentioned, this portal/façade/forecourt element in tomb design is not a conspicuous feature of passage graves. Elsewhere in mainland Europe excavation has revealed offerings of pottery left outside the entrances to passage graves, and at the cruciform sites in Ireland there are significant structures there, but in Britain the record of activity at this point is thin.

11. East Kennet long mound, Wiltshire. (Photograph Aubrey Burl.)

The final covering mound is perhaps the most difficult element of these tombs to interpret. Early scholars debated whether or not it was always present; nowadays it is assumed that it was universal, but the stage at which it was built may still be subject to discussion. Evidence from wooden sites such as Nutbane, Haddenham and Street House demonstrates convincingly that the mound was not built until the chamber and other standing structures had been deliberately demolished and burnt; at stone monuments it is assumed that the cairns were necessary for support and were consequently built hand in hand with the chamber. This would certainly be true where much dry-stone walling was used but the occasional presence of bone outside the chambers and the patent survival of exposed megalithic structures suggest that this assumption should not be accepted uncritically. In passage graves, however, the very existence of the passage as part of the primary structure must imply the presence of the mound.

The lifespan of a wooden building would not be very long – short in comparison with the thousand-year period of veneration evidenced at some stone monuments – but at Nutbane it is clear that there are two phases of building (figure 14), so the period of use must cover a few generations at least. During this time wooden chambers were usually surrounded by an enclosure of some kind. Some were quite small; others were much larger than necessary and became the kerb or boundary to the final mound. There are some monuments – the banked mortuary enclosure at Normanton, Wiltshire, and the wooden ones at Balfarg, Scotland – which may be interpreted as exposure or temporary burial sites which have never been completed by the building of a mound.

At most wooden chambers there is evidence for deliberate and very thorough demolition by fire of the burial structure, façade and fore-building, an act immediately followed by covering the smouldering ruins with earth or chalk from adjacent ditches to form the mound. This act would have made any further access to the burial space impossible but the frequent discovery of later pottery in the silted ditches shows that the monuments were not abandoned at this stage.

The stone tombs with open doorways would not be rendered inaccessible by the construction of the cairn, but blocking within forecourts and entrances may have fulfilled the same symbolic purpose. Unfortunately it is seldom possible to identify the stage at which it was put in place. At Gwernvale it could be shown that the blocking had been removed and replaced on several occasions, an option not available with a burnt wooden chamber (figure 39).

The shape of the covering mound may vary considerably. In some traditions the edge is very carefully built and so the shape must have been significant. Passage graves are normally covered with a round mound; the various types of stone and wooden box chambers are normally covered by elongated mounds (though there is a significant group of round mounds in northern England). The long mounds may vary from 14 metres to 125 metres in length – the average is 47 metres; some are oval, some strictly rectangular, and many are trapezoid – wider and probably higher at the eastern end where the burials lie. The trapezoid shape is distinctive and surprisingly widespread in both Britain and northern Europe, where it is thought to reflect the shape of the great wooden farmhouses of the Danubians – the house of the dead echoing that of the living.

The symbolism of the mound may have become more dominant as fewer chambers remained accessible for burial. The discovery of mounds without burials, such as Beckhampton Road and South Street on the Wiltshire chalk, where bones would be well preserved, suggests that the mound was gaining significance in its own right. In the north and the west, where stone tombs were built, the old sites were still viable monuments. They were not burnt down but they might be closed and in several cases, such as Tulach an t'Sionnaich (figure 34.1) and others in north-east Scotland and Pentre Ifan in Wales (figure 28.8), long cairns without burial chambers have been added to monuments with primary chambers already closed.

At Pentre Ifan it can be argued that a stone façade was also added at this stage, indicating that the tomb retained an active ceremonial role, but one which was no longer primarily concerned with burials. Radiocarbon dates from the forecourt at Monamore on Arran suggest that such ceremonies may have continued for a thousand years or more.

5

Dating long barrows and megalithic tombs

The broad date of these monumental tombs has been known for a long time since the absence of metal goods from the burial chambers led early archaeologists to the correct conclusion that they belonged to the stone age. Despite today's more sophisticated dating methods it often remains difficult to be more precise.

The monuments may be dated by their contents: the pottery and flint tools often, but not always, found with the bones in the chambers. But since these tombs were collective, used over several generations, and, in the stone versions at least, were accessible for perhaps centuries, it may be very difficult to know to what point in the history of the monument these finds should be ascribed. Few can be proved to belong to the construction phase.

Since 1950 it has been possible to date organic material through the measurement of radiocarbon decay. Although fresh organic material seldom survives, charcoal, the indestructible residue of burnt wood, is quite often found, either in 'ritual hearths' or the product of deliberate burning of wooden chambers. Such dates can never be precise and there is, as with contents, the same difficulty in ensuring the correct identification of the phase dated. When more sites have been multi-sampled, however, this method should provide a more accurate chronology for the series of wooden chambers (figure 12).

A third approach to dating is provided by the stratigraphic relationships seen in monuments which have been changed or enlarged at different periods. In this way it has been possible to recognise regional priorities and the arrival of new ideas and to gain useful insights into the history of tomb-building, especially in the west. However, such results simply provide a relative sequence and do not indicate an absolute date in years or even centuries BC.

The general conclusion derived from a study of the contents and the available radiocarbon dates is that the wooden chambers in both southern and northern England were being built between 4000 cal BC and 3500 cal BC, some three or four centuries after the appearance of the new farming economy. The dating of the stone tombs in the west is far more difficult because there are very few reliable radiocarbon dates and the contents have been so exposed to disturbance. However, it seems likely that many tombs were being built in this same British early

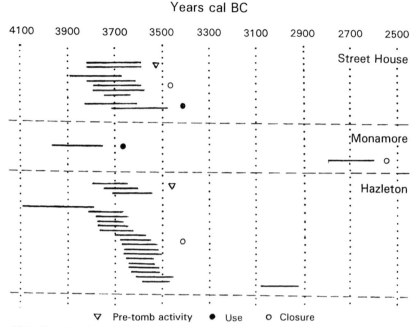

12. Radiocarbon dates from Street House long barrow, Monamore Clyde cairn and Hazleton Cotswold-Severn cairn. The horizontal lines show the possible span of each date (which can never be precise).

neolithic period.

Evidence from well-dated monuments such as Street House (a wooden chamber in North Yorkshire) and Hazleton (a Cotswold-Severn cairn in Gloucestershire) suggest that the period over which burials might be added to the chamber is relatively short, perhaps only two or three centuries. The number of burials at large monuments such as West Kennet in Wiltshire – relatively few in population terms – would tend to confirm this impression.

On the other hand, the regular discovery of British middle neolithic pottery in the silting ditches of long barrows and the late dates for hearths in the forecourts of megalithic tombs like Monamore on Arran indicate that the community's interest in these monuments was maintained over many centuries, even after burial had ceased. The addition of 'blind mounds' as at Tulach an t'Sionnaich, Caithness (figure 34.1), leads to the same conclusion.

In some traditions, mainly in the south of England (wooden long barrow chambers and Cotswold-Severn cairns), monuments were deliberately closed. The point at which this happened is often uncertain. Demolished wooden chambers cannot have been reopened; stone ones like Gwernvale, Breconshire, certainly were. The stone chamber at West Kennet seems to have been accessible for many centuries but was finally completely filled in at a date close to 2400 cal BC (figure 45). In the west blocking is often found in forecourts, suggesting a decision to cease ceremonial activity, but the frequent presence of more than one such layer shows that decisions may not have been final and normally the moment of abandonment is difficult to pinpoint.

It cannot be shown that any new monuments were being built in southern England after about 3000 cal BC though old ones might be maintained. In the north-west it is probable that old traditions lasted longer. The superimposition of a passage grave of classic plan upon a henge monument at Bryn Celli Ddu in Anglesey demonstrates that the traditional dark enclosed grave chamber remained the preferred religious focus there, even though new open-air centres were already being built in the region. Such sequential evidence is not available elsewhere but the uneven distribution of late neolithic single graves – the harbingers of a new attitude in society – suggests that in many western areas the old ideas died hard.

6
Mounds with wooden chambers

The use of wooden posts to build chambers and of chalk or turves for covering mounds must have been largely dictated by availability, but the choice of these materials does predicate certain patterns which make it convenient to discuss these southern and eastern monuments, often called *unchambered*, *earthen* or *non-megalithic long barrows*, separately from the stone tombs of the west.

Southern English long barrows

Evidence for some two hundred long barrows survives in the south of England, the greatest concentration being in the counties of Wiltshire, Dorset and Hampshire, the area known in archaeological literature as 'Wessex'. Within this area certain clusters may be recognised: along the Dorset Ridgeway (twenty-one), on Cranborne Chase (thirty-eight), around Avebury (ten and ten stone tombs) and on Salisbury Plain (eighty-two). Another group of ten may be recognised on the Sussex Downs; elsewhere the distribution is more dispersed.

The frequent clustering of tombs around causewayed enclosures has led to the attractive suggestion that we might recognise in these regions of dense occupation the foci of later chiefdoms. Unfortunately the virtual absence here of evidence for normal domestic settlement makes the hierarchy (family-lineage-tribe) less demonstrable than we might wish.

These earth and chalk mounds have suffered a great deal from later agriculture and very few survive in anything like their original impressive form. The Pimperne long barrow, Dorset, is one which still dominates its surroundings, being 108 metres long and 27.5 metres wide at the east end, where it is 2.4 metres high; it slopes away to a narrower west end. The sizes of the mounds vary a good deal: several are about 100 metres long but the majority in all parts of England are between 26 and 50 metres long. The orientation is almost invariably east-west with a little more latitude allowed in Wessex than elsewhere. The east end is often wider, covering the burial space (where identified). Where excavation has revealed a built edge to the mound it is often decidedly wedge-shaped, but it is difficult to establish this on eroded, unexcavated sites, so it is impossible to say exactly how many were designed in this way.

The internal structures may be revealed by excavation but only relatively few sites have provided good information about the burial structures within. The details differ at each site but the burial space is always a narrow rectangle defined by either pits or posts at front and back. The

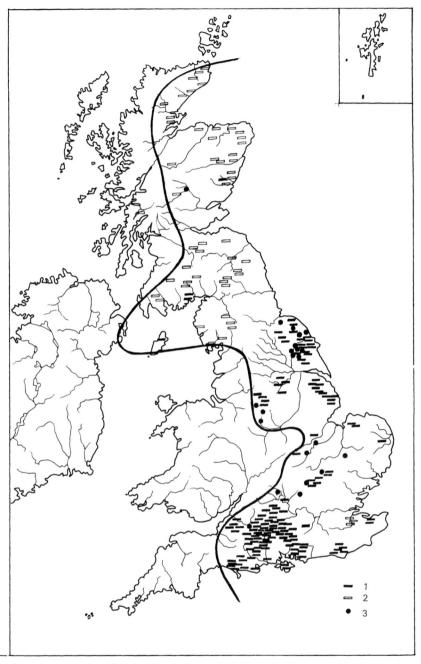

13. Distribution of non-megalithic monuments: 1, earthen long barrows; 2, long stone cairns without evidence of a stone chamber; 3, round mounds. (After Kinnes with adaptations.)

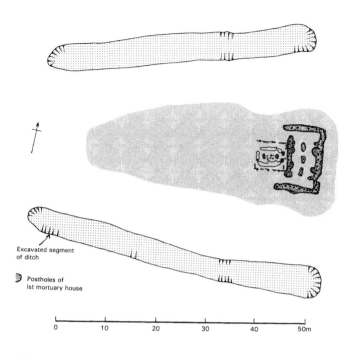

14. Plan of Nutbane long barrow, Hampshire. (After Vatcher, 1959.)

nature of the sides is more problematical and the presence of a roof is often doubtful. The well-preserved waterlogged chamber at Hadden-ham, Cambridgeshire, is a long closed box with floor, sides and roof of large planks supported by three deeply set axial posts and clay banks to either side (figure 8). This pattern can be recognised at other less complete sites, but at Wayland's Smithy, Oxfordshire, the partly stone chamber seems to have been built like a tent (figure 15), while at Nutbane, Hampshire, and probably at Fussell's Lodge, Wiltshire, the space seems to have been unroofed, the bones simply covered by branches or stones (figure 16). At Thickthorn Down, Dorset, the chamber was built entirely of turves. The chambers vary in length from 2 to 6 metres and they are normally about 1 metre wide. The height is uncertain but Haddenham was little more than 1 metre high, making access to the back very awkward unless the roof could be lifted.

The burial chamber is normally enclosed by a wooden fence, perhaps to prevent unauthorised disturbance. The enclosure at Nutbane is small, but at most other sites it is large and defines the space later occupied by the

15. Wayland's Smithy, Oxfordshire: the mortuary structure of the long barrow from the south (see also figure 40). Note the angled stones. (Photograph R. J. C. Atkinson.)

mound. These fences were normally close-set palisades and the depth of the foundations suggests that they were high, certainly in the front where there is usually a straight façade on either side of the chamber. Where the enclosure is not complete the façade may project backwards a short way.

Postholes in front of the façade at some sites indicate the presence of a third structural element – a forebuilding or mortuary house. The forms vary: at Nutbane, exceptionally behind, rather than in front of the façade, a small square building was replaced by a larger one reconstructed as having a gabled roof (figure 14); at both Fussell's Lodge (figure 16) and Wayland's Smithy (figures 15 and 40.2) the posts were substantial and arranged in a trapezoid plan; at Wor Barrow there seemed to be a square porch; at Haddenham two lines of posts projected in front of the façade like antennae (figure 14). The interpretation of these posts as porches, free-standing towers or extra façades is very uncertain and their role is unknown but may have something to do with the prior exposure of bodies. This element is characteristic of southern Britain; it is not regularly present elsewhere.

The multiple inhumations in these southern long barrows are often very well preserved and, since they provide the best evidence for burial rituals in Britain, they have been fully described in chapter 3. No grave goods are found and even broken pottery is rare.

The lifespan of a wooden building is relatively short but the extension of the burial space and the replacement of the original mortuary house at Nutbane suggest quite a long period of use. The decision to close the monument is a definite and final one in this tradition. In many cases the wooden chambers are burnt and in all they are rendered inaccessible by the construction of the mound. This event is particularly vividly recorded at Nutbane, where the chalk of the mound was scorched as it covered the smouldering timbers.

The mound was built from earth or chalk quarried from adjacent ditches. These substantial ditches normally lie to either side, parallel to

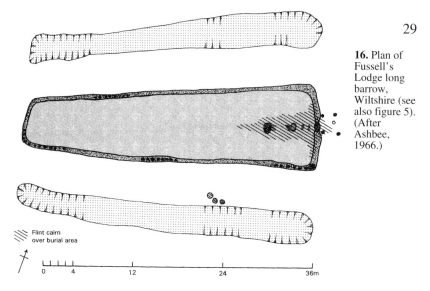

16. Plan of Fussell's Lodge long barrow, Wiltshire (see also figure 5). (After Ashbee, 1966.)

Flint cairn over burial area

the mound, but in Cranborne Chase they are often linked into a U and may sometimes entirely surround it. The mounds themselves were carefully constructed, often containing axial and lateral fences presumably designed to ensure stability and precision of shape. It is the mound which is the lasting monument and the presence of at least three cenotaphs or empty mounds among the Wessex long barrows shows that it developed an independent significance.

The date of these monuments is discussed in chapter 5. The lack of

17. Reconstruction of the mound at Fussell's Lodge. The 'porch' may not have been standing at this stage. (Drawing by Elizabeth Meikle from Ashbee, 1966.)

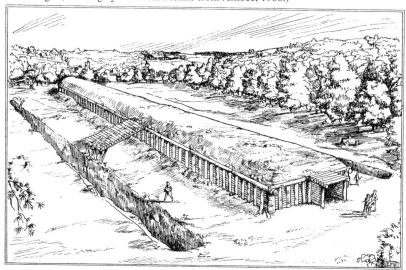

artefacts and the individuality of structural detail revealed by excavation have not favoured arguments about typological development within the southern English group. Suggestions that shorter long barrows may be either earlier or later than the main series have not been convincingly sustained.

Northern English long barrows

The northern English series of long barrows is represented by fifty-four monuments on the chalk wolds of Lincolnshire (fourteen) and Yorkshire (thirty) with a few mounds in Derbyshire and the Lake District. The greatest concentration is around the Great Wold Valley but the region appears to lack the higher level of co-operative institution represented by the causewayed enclosures in the south. 'Political' structures, therefore, would seem to differ though the religious/burial practices in the two regions have much in common.

Externally there is no difference between the northern and southern long barrows; form and size are comparable. Excavation, however, has revealed differences in the design of façades, and the discovery of burnt bones in the chambers and deposits of occupation debris in the forecourts indicates variations in ceremonial custom.

The northern façades are concave and are structurally separate from any enclosing palisade (figure 18). The increasing depth of the foundation trench approaching the centre suggests that the posts rose high to either side of the hypothetical doorway through which, as in the south, any access would be difficult. The plan of these northern façades defines a forecourt more effectively than the straight southern ones and there is seldom any forebuilding within it, though avenues of widely spaced posts have been found on three occasions. A rearrangement of the standard elements may be involved, for at two recently excavated sites, Kilham and Street House, and at Kilburn, dug by Canon Greenwell in the nineteenth century, a mortuary 'house' (certainly unroofed) was found behind the burial area. The forecourt, however, remained a ceremonial space for in the final stage at Willerby Wold and Kilham earth containing occupation debris (potsherds, flints, bones) was carried in and piled against the façade before it was set alight.

As in the south the burial chambers are narrow rectangles defined by posts or pits, but sometimes, especially in Lincolnshire, they may be placed laterally or separated from the façade. They always have side walls or banks and early excavators believed, perhaps rightly, that the axial posts rose through the mound. Such a design, when set alight, would create a flue and intensify the burning. The condition of the bone heaps, disarticulated groups like those at Wayland's Smithy, suggests that this has happened, for those closest to the entrance are most effectively burnt while those at the far end may be only slightly charred. The presence

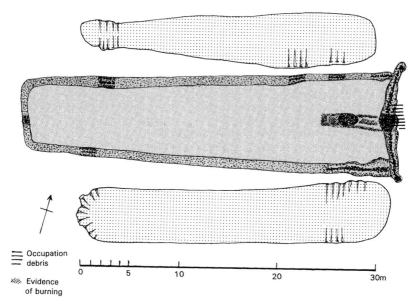

18. Plan of Willerby Wold long barrow, North Yorkshire. (After Manby.)

within the chamber of a layered chalk and wood infill and the regularity of this burning (ten out of fourteen excavated examples on the Yorkshire Wolds) would suggest that it was intentional and these sites are considered to be crematoria, but the preliminary stages (exposure, decomposition and transfer) would seem to be the same as in the south.

The long mounds of the Lake District are built of stone and at Skelmore Heads upright stones appeared to mimic the axial posts of many wooden chambers, even though no bone was found between them. This translation of long barrow features into stone is judged to be very significant and to lie behind the development of many elements of the western megalithic tombs of box-like design.

Long cairns in Scotland

The discovery of wooden chambers under stone cairns is impossible without excavation so the full distribution of such monuments cannot be known. However, some twenty-eight long cairns which show no positive evidence of stone chambers have been recognised in northeastern Scotland and twenty-one are known in southern Scotland. Amongst these are three notable sites, Dalladies in Kincardineshire, and Slewcairn and Lochhill in Wigtownshire (figure 19). All three have

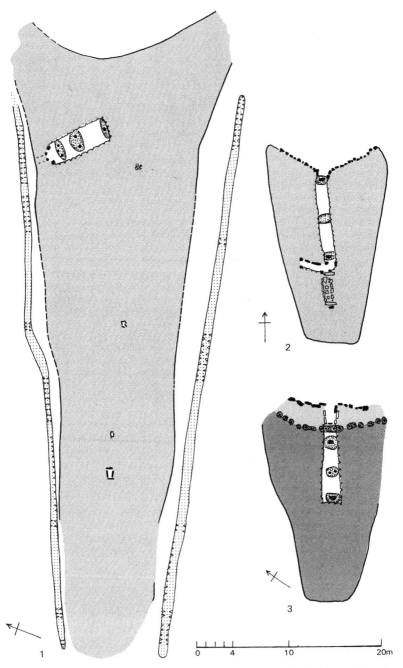

19. Plans of: 1, Dalladies long cairn, Kincardineshire; 2, Slewcairn, Kirkcudbrightshire; 3, Lochhill, Kirkcudbrightshire. (After Piggott and Masters.)

narrow rectangular burial spaces defined by wooden posts and the latter two are especially interesting because stone chambers were built on to them at a later date, thus making manifest the linkage and cross-fertilisation of ideas which can normally only be assumed by typologists.

Although none of the northern cairns has been excavated their presence is significant when the later history of tomb-building in the region is considered. The north of Scotland is an area where the commonest monuments are passage graves in round mounds but evidence from multi-period sites like Tulach an't Sionnaich (figure 34.1) demonstrates that both forms might eventually be used by the same communities. Many of the 'unchambered' cairns and those covering stone chambers have shallow concave forecourts reminiscent of those built in wood in Yorkshire many centuries before.

Wooden chambers under round mounds

Large round earthen barrows are traditionally believed to date from the bronze age, but nineteenth-century excavators in Yorkshire recognised that several covered deposits indistinguishable from those under neighbouring long barrows. While it is probable that some of these were, in truth, damaged long barrows, modern re-excavation and the occasional presence of a circular kerb or ditch have confirmed that the round mound was certainly an acceptable variant from an early date in the north-east of England.

Some forty round mounds can be shown to cover earlier neolithic multiple burials with very limited accompanying goods. At Callis Wold, East Yorkshire (figure 20), and Seamer Moor, North Yorkshire, foundation trenches for wooden façades and enclosures and the concentration of burials within a linear zone suggest that the original burial chambers were identical to those under long barrows. Simpler burial spaces, defined just by a bracketing pair of pits or posts, are rather more common and more widespread, being represented beneath the strange round cairn at Pitnacree, Perthshire, and at Aldwincle, Northamptonshire, where a succession of structures was built.

The kidney-shaped mound at Whiteleaf, Buckinghamshire (figure 20), covered a simple wooden chamber defined by four corner posts which is very reminiscent of early stone tombs such as the Clyde chambers, several of which were originally covered by small round cairns. Such variation of material, chamber and cairn shape occurs very widely in time and space and, where small numbers preclude the recognition of well-defined patterns, it is difficult to make much useful comment. The odd stone chambers and multi-phase cairns of Long Low and Great Ayton Moor and the four megalithic tombs in Derbyshire are a case in point (figure 41.4). It is difficult to know whether they represent

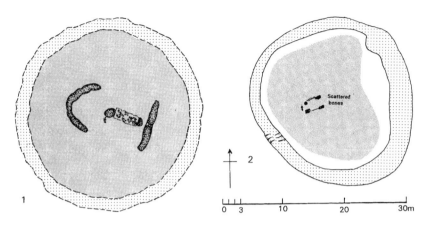

20. Plans of: 1, Callis Wold round barrow, East Yorkshire; 2, Whiteleaf barrow, Buckinghamshire. (After Mortimer/Coombs and Childe and Smith.)

independent local manifestations or far-flung 'satellites' of groups more firmly established elsewhere.

One pattern which emerges significantly from a study of the neolithic round mounds of northern England is the gradually developing custom of leaving personal goods with the dead. At first the range is limited, but by the late neolithic a consistent group of both functional and ceremonial objects may be found, especially in Yorkshire, where the round barrow, for long an acceptable option, becomes the norm. These developments hold within them the germ of many of the most characteristic features of subsequent bronze age burials.

7

Megalithic tombs

The large stone tombs make a greater impact on us today than their wooden counterparts because they remain a fascinating element of our own landscape. Because farmers and wall-builders have, over the years, removed the covering mounds, internal chambers are visible, so we can recognise regional designs and discuss structural details even from unexcavated sites. Consequently the following discussion will be organised into regional and typological groups in a very approximate chronological order.

Clyde cairns

This group consists of about a hundred sites distributed on either side of the Clyde estuary, with notable concentrations in Arran and Kintyre and some significant outliers in Galloway and the Outer Hebrides. The group includes both simple single boxes and more complex compartmentalised monuments with imposing façades. It can be argued that they represent a typological sequence, in the later stages incorporating ideas borrowed from adjacent regions such as the north of Ireland.

Typological theory suggests that the earliest monuments are the simplest. Confirmation of this is derived, not from absolute dating, but from analysis of certain excavated monuments where a sequence of construction can be postulated. From a study of sites such as Mid Gleniron I and II, Wigtownshire, and Cairnholy II, Kirkcudbrightshire, the primary form can be isolated: a stone box, about 2 metres by 1 metre and 1 metre high formed from three or four large slabs (figure 22). At Mid Gleniron this simple chamber was open and accessible; at Cairnholy it was closed and higher stones stood in front so that the roof was set at an angle (figure 9). Access to such closed chambers might involve raising the roof slab. Such stone boxes have a remarkable resemblance to the preserved wooden chamber at Haddenham and the similarity of the early stages of the stone series throughout the Irish Sea province and the wooden chambers is being increasingly stressed. The addition of a simple stone box in front of the wooden chamber and façade at the hybrid long barrow/Clyde cairn at Lochhill, Kirkcudbrightshire (figure 19.3), underlines the connection.

Developments at Mid Gleniron and Cairnholy epitomise the history of the group as a whole. At Mid Gleniron I the simple primary chambers were in small independent cairns. When a third chamber was built between them they were all covered with a long cairn and a façade was

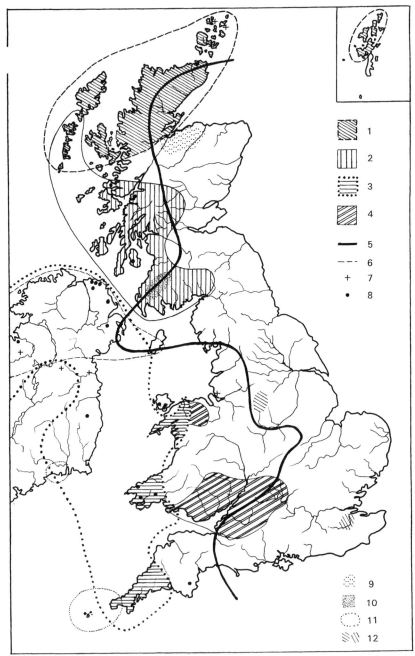

21. Distribution of regional groups of megalithic tombs: 1, Scottish passage graves; 2, Clyde tombs; 3, Portal dolmens (Britain and Ireland); 4, Cotswold-Severn cairns; 5, Boundary of non-megalithic mound distribution; 6, Court tombs (Ireland); 7, Isolated short-passage passage graves; 8, Cruciform passage graves; 9, Clava cairns; 10, Bargrennan tombs; 11, Entrance graves (Britain and Ireland); 12, Stone chambers in Derbyshire and Kent.

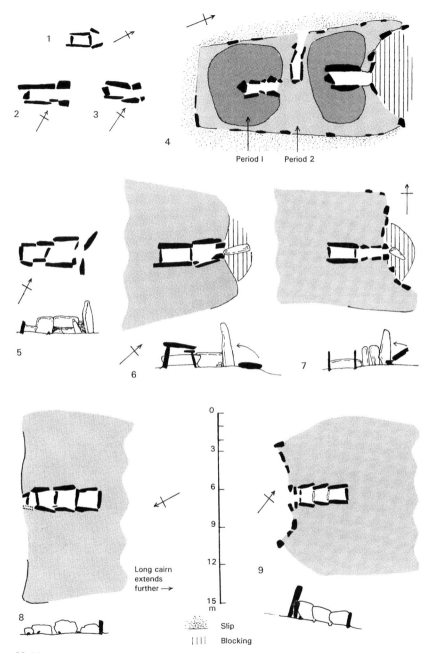

22. Plans of Clyde tombs: 1, Ardmarnock, Argyll; 2, Ardnadam, Argyll; 3, Loch Nell South, Argyll; 4, Mid Gleniron I, Wigtownshire; 5, Brackley, Argyll; 6, Cairnholy II, Kirkcudbright-shire; 7, Cairnholy I, Kirkcudbrightshire; 8, Beacharra, Kintyre; 9, Monamore, Arran. (After Henshall and Scott.)

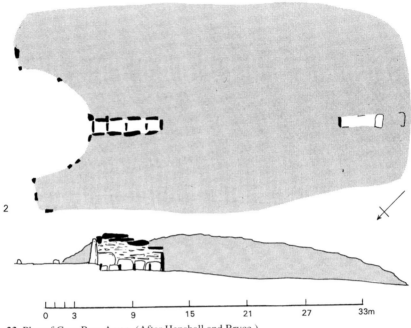

23. Plan of Carn Ban, Arran. (After Henshall and Bryce.)

added to the terminal chamber. At Cairnholy I and II the original chambers (both closed boxes) were extended by the addition of an outer compartment with high portal stones; at Cairnholy I a splendid semi-circular façade was added to either side of the portals (figure 22.7).

The extension of the original box is the common solution to the need for more burial space and tombs were eventually built with two or more compartments, their side stones overlapping and separated by only a low sill, as at Beacharra, Argyll (figure 22.8). Beacharra is a gallery of uniform height, but usually the entrance is marked by tall stones. On the higher ground of Arran and Kintyre tombs which are likely to represent a later expansion of settlement have their entrances embellished by high façades which define deep semicircular forecourts (figures 23 and 26). This architectural device, featuring on the later tombs, is thought to be borrowed from the northern Irish court tombs. It is also found occasionally as an addition to Hebridean passage graves (figure 31.6) and is indicative of a British middle neolithic phase of contact and exchange in the northern Irish Sea region, although the early wooden façades of Yorkshire may have an ancestral role at a further remove.

The hypothesis that these tombs develop towards multiple chambers

24. (Left) Small Clyde chamber with low portals and fallen lintel, Loch Nell South, Dalineun, Argyll (see plan, figure 22). (Crown copyright: Royal Commission on the Ancient and Historical Monuments of Scotland.)

25. (Right) Clyde cairn with high portals fronting a single chamber, Adam's Grave, Ardnadam, Argyll (see plan, figure 22). (Crown copyright: Royal Commission on the Ancient and Historical Monuments of Scotland.)

and increasing emphasis on the entrance is an attractive one accepted by most scholars but it must be admitted that it is based to a dangerous extent upon a recognition of multi-period building which was not noted by all the original excavators. Moreover the exposure of the stone chambers has made the problem of dating the contents particularly difficult and there are no radiocarbon dates for any of the putatively early monuments.

The chambers contain disarticulated bones, inhumations and true cremations, that is, bones burnt elsewhere and brought into the chamber as ashes. In the Irish Sea province cremation was an option from an early date: at Nether Largie, Argyll, the cremations preceded the inhumations; at Brackley, also in Argyll, it was the other way round. In the Clyde, in contrast to other regions, intact pots were placed in the tombs. The excavator of Beacharra thought that the three compartments had been used in succession, the innermost one first, but the evidence is insufficient to show that this was a regular practice.

The Isle of Man

The Isle of Man contains several very impressive megalithic tombs, like Cashtal yn Ard and King Orry's Grave, which share features with

26. East Bennan, Arran, from the back: a Clyde cairn with four-compartment chamber and façade. (Photograph Aubrey Burl.)

the Clyde cairns and the court tombs of northern Ireland. The monument at Ballafayle is particularly interesting as it appears, like Lochhill, to combine wooden and stone structures.

Bargrennan group

This group is composed of about a dozen rather disparate monuments in Galloway and Ayrshire. They normally have rectangular chambers, but with a passage element, and are covered by circular cairns (figure 41.2). They occur within the territory of the Clyde cairns and their end chambers are similar; however, the passage and a preference for round

27. Carnedd Hengwm South, Merioneth, a portal dolmen, showing the portal, closing slab and lower side stone of the chamber behind. The fallen capstone is in the foreground. The northern side of the chamber has gone.

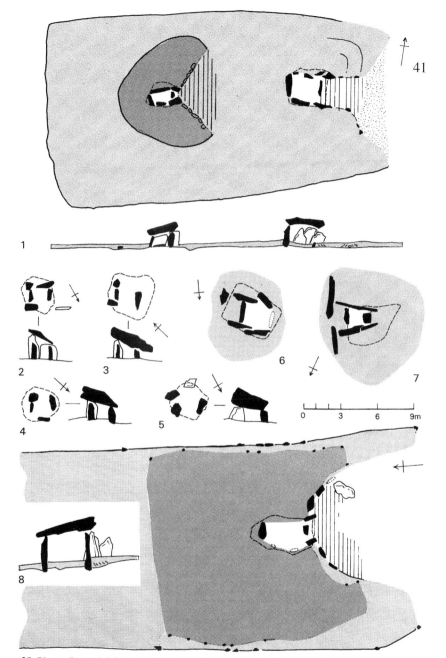

41

28. Plans of portal dolmens in Wales and Cornwall: 1, Dyffryn Ardudwy, Merioneth, a two-period monument; 2, Gwern Einion, Merioneth; 3, Tan y Muriau west chamber, Lleyn; 4, Carreg Coetan Arthur, Newport, Pembrokeshire; 5, Llech y Dribedd, Pembrokeshire; 6, Trethevy, Cornwall; 7, Zennor Quoit, Cornwall; 8, Pentre Ifan, Pembrokeshire, a two-period cairn (see also front cover). (After Lynch and Todd.)

29. (Left) Dyffryn Ardudwy, Merioneth, west chamber: a portal dolmen from the front (see plan, figure 28). Scale in feet.

30. (Right) Gwern Einion, Merioneth: a portal dolmen from the side, showing the characteristic sloping capstone (see plan, figure 28).

cairns suggest that ideas have also been borrowed from passage-grave builders in the region. They are a puzzling group of uncertain date.

Portal dolmens

These monuments share many of the basic traits of the Clyde cairns and must spring from a similar background. They are, however, much more distinctive and imposing and always retain the single-chamber form. Their most characteristic feature is the high closed entrance formed by an H-shaped arrangement of stones, mutually supportive as in a house of cards so that the closing slab cannot be safely removed. The small rectangular chamber behind is low, so the capstone often lies at a daring angle (figure 30). Only very rarely is there an orthostatic façade but excavation has shown that a forecourt area in front of the entrance is to be expected. Where they survive the cairns may be round or rectangular, but never exceptionally long. On level ground the chamber faces east but on a slope, as they often are, they face uphill.

Portal dolmens may be found on either side of the Irish Sea, in Cornwall, Wales and south-east Ireland. They also occur in the north of Ireland among the court and wedge tombs and Irish scholars have, until recently, believed that they represented the final 'degenerate' form of the court tomb, shrunk to a single chamber without façade or court. However, the evidence of an early date for Dyffryn Ardudwy in Wales has caused this view to be revised and the group is now recognised as a separate, early phenomenon on a par with the Clyde cairns and, like them, having an independent origin in the 'box concept'.

There are only some thirty-five to fifty examples in Wales and south-west England but in some valleys and sub-regions the distribution is locally dense and the style is obviously dominant and likely to represent a stable development over several centuries. In some other areas favourable to early farming, such as Anglesey, no portal dolmens have been found though less distinctive box chambers, such as Trefignath (figure 3), exist side by side with other styles. In south Pembrokeshire, too, differing traditions seem to have co-existed, though whether they were exactly contemporary is uncertain.

The characteristic portal dolmen is a very assured structure and it is likely that the earliest tombs in the region are less distinctive boxes, more like those in Scotland. Though such monuments exist none has been excavated and multi-period sites like Dyffryn Ardudwy and Carnedd Hengwm South in Merioneth and Pentre Ifan in Pembrokeshire have a classic portal dolmen as the primary structure, not a simple chamber like Mid Gleniron. Consequently a typological sequence like that in Scotland is less easy to identify further south, though the addition of a high façade and the extension of the long cairn at Pentre Ifan demonstrates that Wales was equally receptive to new architectural ideas in the middle neolithic.

Portal dolmens tend to be located on lower ground in farmland and consequently excavation of their denuded cairns and chambers is seldom rewarding. The most significant results have come from Dyffryn Ardudwy in Merioneth, excavated in 1960-2, when two periods of construction were recognised and the earlier, classic portal dolmen was dated by the discovery of typologically early shouldered bowls used in ceremonies at the blocking of its forecourt (figure 28.1). The later eastern chamber lacks the classic high closed front, a fact which should prompt caution in identifying all simple chambers as early. The lack of primary burials at Dyffryn is unfortunate because the permanently closed entrance to portal dolmens does raise doubts about their use as communal graves. It would usually be possible to insert bones, if not bodies, over the closing slab but there is no positive evidence of the original burial ritual in this group.

The Cornish portal dolmens – the Penwith group – are slightly different from the Welsh and Irish ones in that they often have two flanking stones set just forward of the portal. The best-preserved example is at Zennor but

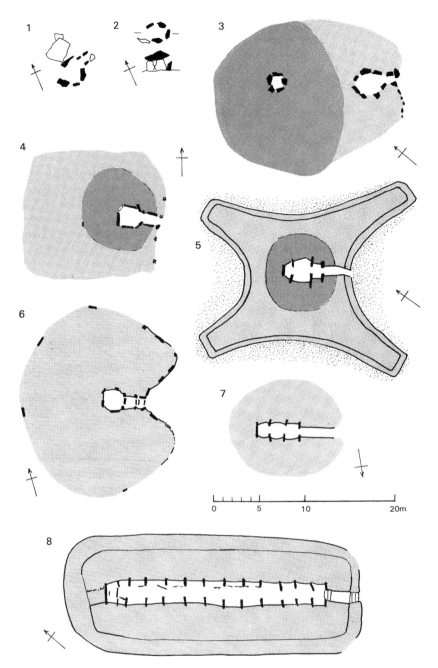

31. Plans of passage graves: 1, Hanging Stone, Burton, Pembrokeshire; 2, Bodowyr, Anglesey; 3, Achnacreebeag, Argyll, a two-period monument; 4, Balvraid, Inverness-shire, a two-period monument; 5, Ormiegill, Caithness; 6, Rhun an' Dunain, Skye; 7, Warehouse West, Caithness; 8, Midhowe, Rousay, Orkney. (After Lynch, Ritchie and Henshall.)

32. A short-passage passage grave, Achnacreebeag, under excavation (see plan, figure 31). (Crown copyright: Royal Commission on the Ancient and Historical Monuments of Scotland.)

the well-known monument at Trethevy also has this regional feature (figure 28.6 and 7). As in Wales, there are a number of simple box-like chambers which might represent the earliest monuments but none has produced any good dating evidence. All the Cornish monuments had been considered late, but this view, derived from Irish typologies, should be revised, especially since neolithic settlements in the far west, where the tombs are concentrated, were occupied in the early neolithic.

Simple passage graves

A passage grave may be defined as a burial chamber, normally polygonal but often rectangular, separated from the outside world by a structurally distinct passage narrower and lower than the chamber. Such monuments are generally covered by round mounds. The burial rituals may involve either cremation or inhumation, and both may be found at some sites. Although passage graves are often placed in conspicuous sites, there is seldom evidence for ceremonial activity outside the passage entrance; rituals may have occurred within the chamber itself. Despite well-known exceptions among later groups such as the cruciform chambers in Ireland, simple passage graves are not regularly found within cemeteries but have a dispersed distribution similar to that of other megalithic tombs in Britain.

The distribution of simple passage graves is widespread in Europe. They are the dominant type in many parts of Iberia and western France. In Brittany those with short passages are generally agreed to be the earlier type and appear at about 4100 cal BC, a horizon later than simple box-like graves beneath long earthen mounds.

In Britain they are arguably an introduced type. Their distribution up the Irish Sea and into Scotland and the Western Isles suggests a link with Brittany and Atlantic Europe. As in Brittany, they are probably not the

33. (Above) Camster Long cairn, Caithness: view of the façade, forecourt and passage entrances (see plan, figure 34). (Photograph James Dyer.)

earliest type of formalised burial, for at Achnacreebeag in Argyll the small passage grave has been added to a mound covering a closed box chamber (figures 31.3 and 32). However, pottery from Broadsands in Devon and Carreg Samson in Pembrokeshire indicates that the type was current in the early neolithic although no reliable radiocarbon dates are available.

In the south Irish Sea province the type does not seem to have been successful; there are only a few widely scattered sites and the style does not become dominant in any sub-region. Nor do simple passage graves become the focus for later additions and modifications even though some tombs, such as Broadsands, Devon, and Ty Newydd in Anglesey, may have been used for a long time. The picture is of a tradition which did not take deep root amongst a population already familiar with other ideas of monumental burial.

In western and northern Scotland and on the Orkney and Shetland islands the story seems to have been very different. Here the simple passage grave with short passage may be seen as the origin of a long tradition of megalithic architecture in which the great stalled cairns of Orkney may be recognised as the final form, stemming from such sites as Balvraid, Inverness, and Embo, Sutherland. However, it is not only the demonstration of a convincing typological sequence, but also the presence of several monuments, for instance Balvraid and Camster Long and Tulach an t'Sionnaich in Caithness, where the small passage grave can be shown to be primary, modified to conform to a variety of new ideas, which gives credence to the view that passage-grave building became the dominant tradition over a wide territory, and there developed its own regional complexities (figures 31 and 34).

The Orkney-Cromarty-Hebrides group

As defined by Audrey Henshall in 1972, this group consists of some three hundred monuments with quite variable chamber and cairn plans, but all having the crucial chamber/passage distinction. The development of the long stalled cairn through the multiplication of jamb stones set

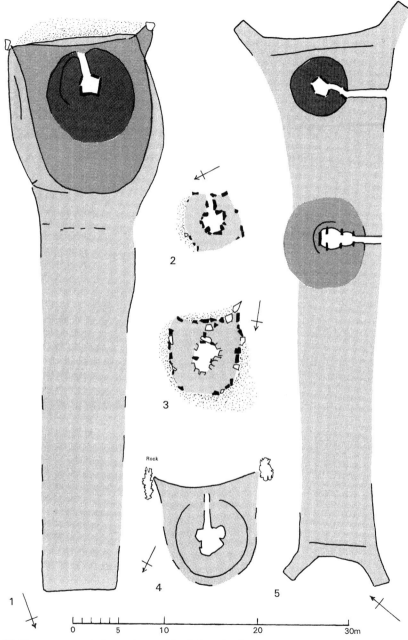

34. Passage graves in long cairns and heel-shaped cairns: 1, Tulach an t'Sionnaich, Caithness; 2, Vementry, Shetland; 3, Hansie's Crooie, Shetland; 4, Pettigarth's Field, Shetland; 5, Camster Long, Caithness. (After Henshall and Masters.)

across the axis of the chamber can be easily seen in the selection of plans in figure 31. Naturally the elongation of the chamber leads to the elongation of the cairn at sites such as Midhowe on Rousay but at others, such as Camster Long, the massive cairn is not functional and must reflect some 'ideological' choice (figure 34.5). Isbister on South Ronaldsay has additional side chambers after the manner of the Maes Howe group of cruciform tombs, an unsurprising exchange of ideas among island communities. On the Shetland islands the passage-grave chamber assumes a trefoil plan and the small cairns are 'heel-shaped', having a slightly concave façade to either side of the entrance (Zetland group, figure 34.2-4). However, these façades do not seem to have attracted much ceremonial activity. In the Orkneys, too, and on the mainland the idea of concave façades on both long and short rectangular cairns is adopted, probably from south-eastern Scotland. In the Hebrides the occasional funnel-shaped façade (figure 31.6) is more reminiscent of the Clyde and Irish court-tomb architecture.

The sequence at Tulach an t'Sionnaich, Caithness (figure 34.1), from simple passage grave, through heel cairn and façade to long cairn, demonstrated by excavation in 1961, is a key to understanding the development, exchange and superimposition of ideas about tomb and cairn building in this part of Britain, where an impressive proportion of the communities' energies must have been put into the work.

The Cotswold-Severn group

This series of 120-30 monuments is unusually diverse in that three different chamber designs and dispositions are included within the group, which is unified only by a strict adherence to a trapezoidal cairn plan, emphasised by an exceptionally careful mound construction and fine external walling. Amongst the well-preserved examples, some fourteen monuments have a complex transepted chamber design with antechamber and passage, off which open one, two or three pairs of chambers, often with a further chamber at the end. Some twenty tombs are characterised by a single terminal chamber of simple design but large dimensions. The third series has chambers set laterally within the cairn, these chambers normally being rectangular with some structural distinction between chamber and passage. In the Cotswold area there are about twenty of this third type with relatively simple chambers entered from either side of the cairn. These laterally chambered cairns preserve an interest in the eastern end by the provision there of a false portal or forecourt.

These monuments occur principally on the Cotswolds between Bristol and Oxford but there is a significant group of seven in the Avebury area, where earthen long barrows were also built. They are also found

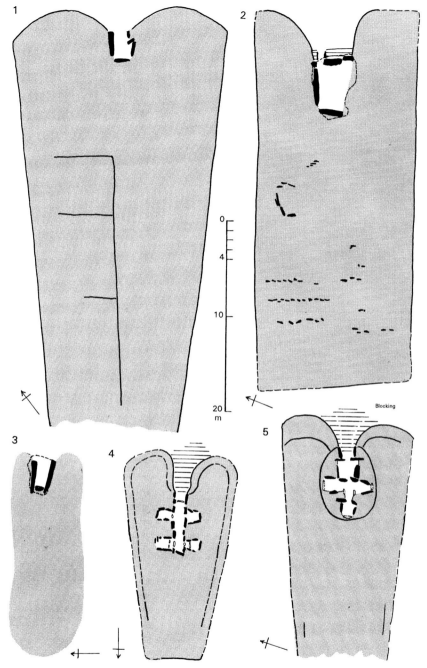

35. Cotswold-Severn cairns: terminal chambers, single and transepted: 1, Randwick, Gloucestershire; 2, Tinkinswood, Glamorgan; 3, St Lythans, Glamorgan; 4, Parc le Breos Cwm, Glamorgan; 5, Nympsfield, Gloucestershire. (After Corcoran, Saville and RCAHMW.)

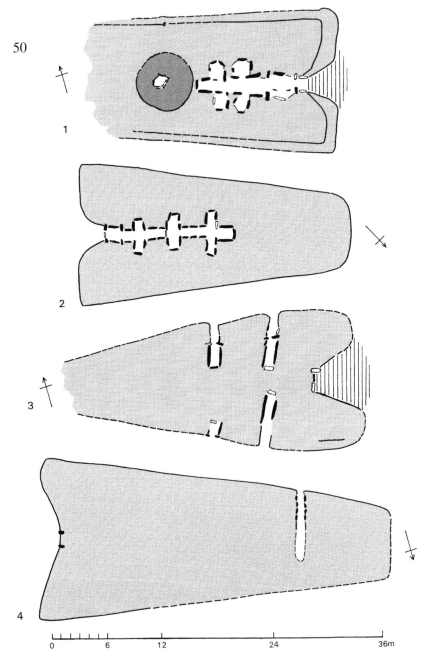

36. Cotswold-Severn cairns: transepted and lateral chambers: 1, Notgrove, Gloucestershire; 2, Stoney Littleton, Somerset; 3, Luckington, Wiltshire; 4, West Tump, Gloucestershire. (After Corcoran.)

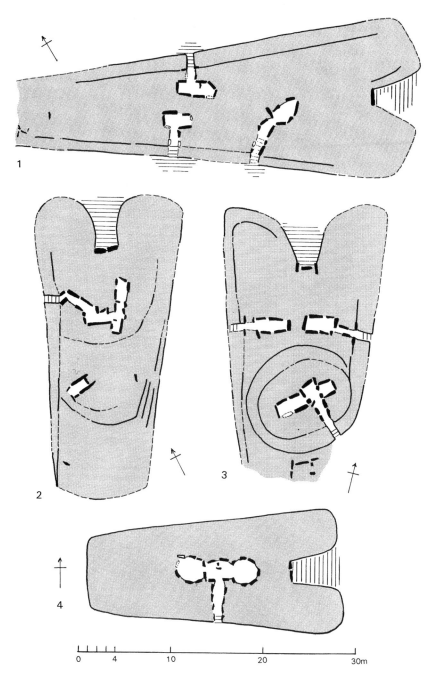

37. Cotswold-Severn cairns in Wales: 1, Gwernvale, Breconshire; 2, Pipton, Breconshire; 3, Ty Isaf, Breconshire; 4, Capel Garmon, Conwy. (After Britnell and Lynch.)

38. Transepted chamber, Nympsfield, Gloucestershire (see plan, figure 35). (Photograph James Dyer.)

on the northern shores of the Severn estuary, where about a dozen lie between Gower and Chepstow. In all these areas there are monuments of all three types; in the Usk valley, Breconshire, in a region centring upon Talgarth, there are ten to fourteen tombs of only one type, a complex lateral design, with both simple and transepted chambers and false portals and forecourts (figure 37). In north Wales there are a few isolated examples of Breconshire type, such as Carnedd Hengwm North and Capel Garmon, an indication of the spread of these architectural/religious ideas into areas where previously very different monuments had been built.

Such complex structures have been the subject of a great deal of argument about typological development, the origin of the design features and the possibility of multi-period development. Meticulous excavation

39. Blocking deposits in and around the north chamber, Gwernvale, Breconshire. Note the inner and outer dry-stone walls (see plan, figure 37). (Photograph Bill Britnell.)

of the carefully built cairns has shown that the latter possibility (so fruitful of understanding in the other groups) is very seldom an option with Cotswold-Severn cairns; the complex ground plans are designed as a unit.

The theory of typological development, much favoured until 1969, argued that the terminally transepted type, introduced from the Vendée area of western France, was primary and that the laterally arranged chambers represented a break-up of that original idea, those with false portals like Belas Knap and West Tump being closer to the original than those, like Hazleton North, with only a forecourt (figures 36.4 and

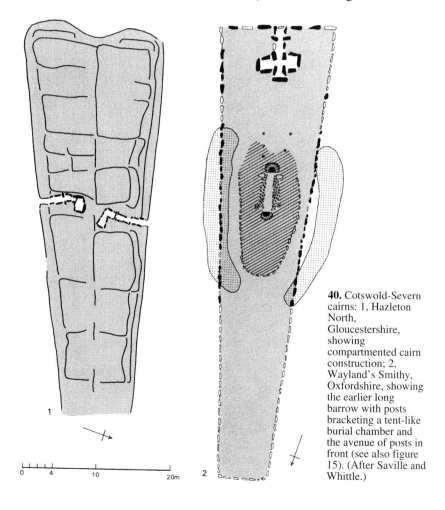

40. Cotswold-Severn cairns: 1, Hazleton North, Gloucestershire, showing compartmented cairn construction; 2, Wayland's Smithy, Oxfordshire, showing the earlier long barrow with posts bracketing a tent-like burial chamber and the avenue of posts in front (see also figure 15). (After Saville and Whittle.)

40.1). This logically attractive view presupposes a chronological primacy for the terminally transepted cairns which unfortunately has not been substantiated.

In 1969 John Corcoran challenged this developmental orthodoxy and suggested that the three different chamber arrangements should be regarded as independent and contemporary styles. The lateral chambers could be compared to passage graves in long cairns such as Barnenez in northern Brittany, while the comparison with transepted passage graves in the Vendée would remain valid for sites such as Nympsfield, Gloucestershire, and Stoney Littleton, Somerset (figures 35 and 36). The simple terminal chambers might be a local example of the general 'box idea' and in any case the unifying element of the trapezoid cairn, constructed with exceptional care and precision in this region, where the use of dry-stone walling provided an ideal medium, could be linked to the long-barrow tradition where mounds were very often trapezoid and defined by stout palisades. The two traditions overlap in the Avebury region and the connection was conclusively demonstrated at Wayland's Smithy in Oxfordshire, where a Cotswold-Severn tomb succeeded and overlaid a long barrow with wooden chamber (figure 40.2).

Excavations since the mid 1970s have tended to confirm the view that the three chamber designs are broadly contemporary, and, if anything, the lateral ones are slightly earlier. Discussion of origins and foreign contacts has been more circumspect. The elaborate transepted design still finds its closest analogues in France, amongst the developed passage graves of the west coast which belong to an horizon of about 3800 cal BC. The lateral cairns, with paired chambers approached from either side, differ somewhat from Breton single-sided long cairns with passage graves, but the slightly earlier chronological horizon would be appropriate. As the complementarity of wooden and stone structures is increasingly recognised, the link between southern English long barrows and the Cotswold-Severn cairns has been generally accepted.

Radiocarbon dates for six Cotswold-Severn cairns are available. They suggest that lateral cairns in the Cotswolds and Breconshire were being built about 3500 cal BC and the transepted chambers were in use some two or three hundred years later, a view supported by the appearance of decorated pottery in transepted chambers, but only in the blocking of lateral cairns. Like other megalithic tombs, they belong, therefore, to the earlier part of the British neolithic but the complex mixture of ideas expressed in their architecture suggests that they represent a second stage, an amalgamation between established mound-building traditions and introduced burial-chamber designs. They do not seem to have very much in common with the simple passage graves of the Irish Sea coasts, which are almost certainly earlier, but their ancestry must lie in the same regions. The significance of stratigraphically early structures such as the 'rotunda' at Notgrove is uncertain.

The link with southern English long barrows is emphasised by the similarity of burial rituals. Bones have been surprisingly well preserved in several Cotswold-Severn tombs and their analysis leads to the same conclusions: multiple inhumations added successively to the chamber and disturbed, rearranged and occasionally removed for ritual use elsewhere. The discovery of final burials still in articulation at Lanhill (figure 6) and Hazleton North suggests that it was not customary to leave the body to decay in some other place, although the constricted access to some stone chambers would suggest that this would have been a more practical option.

Another point of similarity with long barrows is the custom of formal closure. Blocking is regularly found in the outer passageways and, where evidence allows, it can be shown that the entrance has been most carefully concealed by knitting back the dry-stone walling of the outer revetment. In some cairns the chamber entrances have been blocked by additional stone piled against the revetment (figure 39), and some have argued that the whole of the cairn has been deliberately despoiled by pulling down the revetment, in an act which may be considered parallel to the burning of the wooden chamber at many long barrows.

Radiocarbon dates from the bones at Hazleton North (figure 12) suggest that the burial period there was short, a conclusion which is in line with rather less secure evidence from most other sites. However, the opening and reopening of chambers at Gwernvale, Breconshire, and the undoubted late neolithic date of the final filling of the chambers at West Kennet, Wiltshire, demonstrate that the cessation of active burial need not imply the abandonment of the monument. Like northern tombs which were changed and modified in later centuries, the period of veneration for some Cotswold-Severn cairns could have spanned the entire neolithic period.

Kent group

The Medway valley, where large sarsen stones may be found, contains five long cairns; Kit's Coty House is the best-known. They are kerbed and have an exceptionally large rectangular stone chamber at the east end; at Addington the bones of twenty-two individuals were found in this chamber. The monuments clearly belong to a neolithic tradition but they are separated geographically from other British groups and many scholars suggest that they are more plausibly linked to the long kerbed mounds of Holland and north Germany. Another view is that they are stone versions of the more familiar southern wooden chambers.

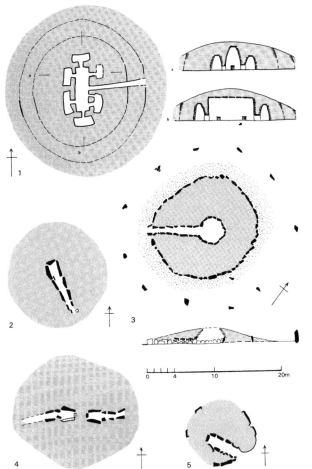

41. 1, Quanterness, Orkney: plan and sections of the passage grave of Maes Howe type. 2, Bargrennan, Kirkcudbrightshire: plan of cairn. 3, Corrimony, Inverness-shire: plan and section of the Clava cairn. 4, Fivewells, Derbyshire: plan of cairn. 5, Pennance, Cornwall: plan of entrance grave. (After Henshall, Ward and Daniel.)

Entrance graves of Cornwall and Scilly

These monuments are simple wedge-shaped galleries beneath relatively small round cairns. The chambers are of uniform height but are wider at the back than at the entrance, which may be blocked by a sill stone (figure 41.5). The frequent discovery of bronze age urns in the cairns and the absence of any earlier neolithic material amongst the cremation burials has led to these tombs being dated to the later neolithic. Such a consistently late date is rare amongst megalithic tombs and is an indication that here in the far west, as in Anglesey, the old traditions survived much longer than in most parts of Britain.

There are about twenty sites in Cornwall, in an area where portal dolmens were built, but the other fifty or more surviving examples are found on the Scilly Islands, then a larger landmass than at present. A small group in south-east Ireland, near Tramore, may be related.

Cruciform passage graves

These impressive and complex structures, enriched with mural art, are characteristic of Ireland, where they were being built from about 3500 cal BC. A few notable examples occur on the eastern side of the Irish Sea: at Barclodiad y Gawres in Anglesey, Calderstones in Liverpool and, most famously, at Maes Howe on Orkney. It is on Orkney that the style takes deepest root and a group of ten other monuments of this type can be found (figure 41.1). They are judged to belong to the later phases of the neolithic there.

In Ireland and Anglesey, beneath a large round mound is a central chamber, entered by a long passage and having a high corbelled roof, off which open three low side chambers in a cruciform plan. In Orkney, where the use of fine sandstone gives the dry-walled chambers an extra sophistication, the tombs develop more complex plans, with up to fourteen side chambers. However, they lack the decoration which is such a fascinating element in the Irish and Welsh examples (figure 42). This decoration is pecked into the surface of wall and roof stones and at Newgrange, Dowth and Knowth, County Meath, also occurs on the kerbstones around the edge of the mound. Spiral and zigzag motifs appear regularly but the designs are entirely abstract and their meaning remains elusive.

Clava cairns

These twelve round cairns occur in a restricted area around Inverness in north-east Scotland and, despite the simplicity of their circular chambers and shortish passages, they are judged to be a late manifestation of the tomb-building tradition. This is because the kerbed cairn is regularly surrounded by a free-standing circle of stones carefully graduated in height, the tallest opposite the entrance on the south-west side (figure 41.3). These features also appear at bronze age ring cairns in the same region and it is judged that these structural similarities must imply a similarity of date.

8

Understanding monumental tombs
and their role

It must be admitted from the outset that the title of this chapter is an aspiration which cannot be definitively fulfilled. We will never understand all the pressures and subtleties of motivation which led to the sacrifice of time and resources, to the choice of design and to the selection of site; nor will we be able to recognise all the changes which may have affected the community's perception of the monument through the centuries. However, there are certain topics which we may usefully consider in this connection, while remembering that this is an area in which factual information is deficient, where theory rules and where current views may be expected to change at the behest of historiographical fashion.

The tombs are the product of deliberate social behaviour: therefore, we may expect their distribution and size to tell us something about the society of the people who built them.

The first question that might be asked is: 'Are there any farming groups in Britain who did not build large tombs?' The absence of tombs in some areas of early agriculture such as south-eastern England would suggest that in Britain, as in southern and eastern Europe, the answer is: 'Yes, but they are rare.'

The virtual invisibility of settlement in southern Britain, whether homesteads or villages, makes it difficult to discuss the location of the tombs in relation to the houses of the living. However, such evidence as we have (mainly from Ireland and the west) suggests that the village on the central European scale is unknown and that the isolated farmstead or hamlet is the normal unit of settlement. Similarly, the tombs are scattered; though pairs may occur, especially in the Cotswolds, they never form cemeteries.

Such a dispersed pattern is believed to reflect 'segmentary societies' – communities of equivalent size, status and economy operating independently within their own lands. Such communities might belong to a single kinship group or perhaps emcompass more. In most areas of Britain the density of tombs is not unlike that of later parish churches, which would suggest that several families were involved. In other countries, Portugal for instance, the distribution can be very much more dense, suggesting that they relate to smaller units of land and perhaps a single nuclear family. Such variations show that, though we may believe that all monumental tombs share a broadly similar significance, the

42. Reconstruction of the ritual performed within the decorated passage grave, Barclodiad y Gawres, Anglesey. (By permission of the National Museum of Wales.)

development of that role is far from uniform.

Because bones are nearly always found within the chambers and because these bones represent what could be family groups, it is believed that the veneration and power of ancestors are central to the world-view reflected in the monuments. Numerous ethnographic parallels can be cited for the general role of ancestors in the well-being of the living and for several of the particular practices observed.

The physical link with ancestors which is enshrined in the presence of the tomb may have been considered as a guarantee of continuing fertility – of the human family, of their animals and of their land. For farmers the significance of the land, and of their own tract of land in particular, becomes a dominating concern and it is probable that the presence of the tomb within the ancestral lands may have acted as a statement of ownership, a symbol which legitimised succeeding generations.

This role as a territorial marker is difficult to demonstrate. The tombs do not have a convincingly regular relationship to tracts of suitable agricultural land, one per valley or viable land unit, but in broad terms patterns like that surviving on Arran are susceptible to this kind of interpretation (figure 43). The fact that in several instances the exterior of the monument seems to become more significant than the burial chamber also lends some confirmation to this view.

Large though they are, it has been calculated that most of the tombs could have been built by a group of about twenty individuals over a period of a few years during slack seasons in the agricultural year. Such a conclusion provides further support for the idea that the tombs are the

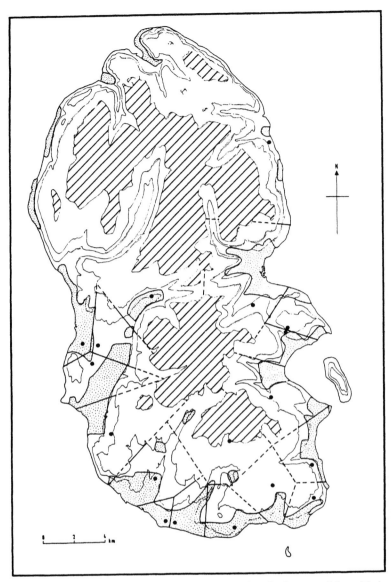

43. Map of Arran showing megalithic tombs and notional territories around them. Modern arable land is stippled; land over 300 metres is hatched. (After Renfrew.)

products of relatively small social units.

The collection of materials may have been the longest job, but it could be spread out over a reasonable time. Bringing in large stones would have necessitated much preparation of the route, the making of long ropes and the felling of trees for rollers. At the final stage the help of neighbours may have been needed. The erection of uprights could have been achieved by the use of wooden levers and fulcra; the positioning of capstones is a more difficult task which may have involved the prior construction of part of the cairn as a ramp, or the use of a lot of wooden scaffolding, for which the evidence has never been found. Where drystone walling and corbelled vaults are employed there were fewer logistical problems, but great skill and experience were needed. The earth and wood chambers may seem easier to erect, but it should not be forgotten that large oak beams can be as heavy as stone.

All this activity, taking workers away from primary production, must have put a strain on the food resources of the community and this is one of the reasons for suggesting that the earliest tombs are likely to have been small. At the other end of the period, it can be shown in some areas such as the Orkneys that only a few significantly larger tombs were being built. Such a development suggests that society was changing, that the original segmentary groups were being centralised, that certain people, perhaps to be categorised as chiefs, though they cannot yet be recognised through personal wealth, were able to call on larger workforces and greater resources.

In southern Britain this stage is not apparent among the tombs but may be recognised in the construction of other public monuments. In the Wessex region the causewayed enclosure, an assembly site which may have played some ill-defined role in both religion and politics (if the two may be separated at this time), had always existed as a focus for groups from a relatively large sub-region. Here these centralising tendencies continued, with the construction of fewer, larger sites – the 'Wessex henges' such as Avebury, Durrington Walls and Mount Pleasant – which had a much reduced burial role. In this region the moment of closure of a tomb, whether wooden or stone, had always been more formal, which suggests that the separation of religion and secular politics may have come earlier, explaining

44. The hierarchy of social aggregation in southern England and in western Britain.

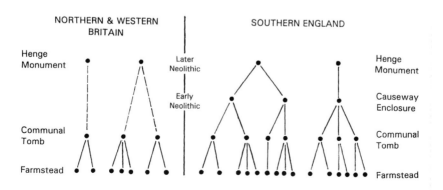

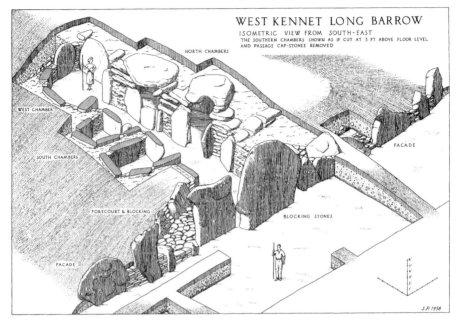

45. An isometric view of the chamber and blocked forecourt at West Kennet cairn, Wiltshire, an instance of formal tomb closure. (From Piggott, 1962.)

perhaps why the new 'chieftain society' found an alternative monument through which to express its power.

Everywhere the stability and community of the earlier neolithic, and its religious certainties characterised by the great monumental tombs, were beginning to crumble during the late neolithic. The new power structures which emerge take different forms in different areas. In the west, as in the Orkneys, the tomb remains significant; in Yorkshire an emphasis on personal belongings and individual burial becomes evident, though the monuments are still communal; in the south the latest use of some communal tombs gives hints of individuality, but it is here that the dominance of burial as an expression of community power seems to be eclipsed and replaced soonest.

In the succeeding bronze age, when rare commodities could be controlled and distributed to followers by those at the centre, the expressions of power change. The link with ancestors is no longer its key and the new graves, the richest of them filled with items of display and with weapons, show us a new elite whose position was dependent on more personal qualities of strength and leadership.

9
Glossary of terms

Articulated bone: bones in the normal anatomical relationship.

Axial: set on the axis or central line of the monument.

Barrow: mound, normally of earth (long barrow, round barrow).

Cairn: mound of stones (long cairn, round cairn).

Cist: box-like grave normally built of four stone slabs.

Danubians: early farming society of south-eastern Europe.

Dolmen: Celtic word used in English to denote a small megalithic chamber.

Forecourt: formalised area in front of the entrance to a tomb; also *blind forecourt*, one without a functional entrance to the tomb.

Gallery graves: group of graves with chambers of uniform height and width; a term rarely used now since the unity of the group is doubted.

Grave goods: personal equipment buried with the dead for use in the afterlife or to show status.

Lateral chamber: burial chamber entered from the side of the mound.

Megalithic: built of large stones (derived from the Greek).

Mesolithic: the middle stone age, a hunting society (*c*.10,000 to 4000 cal BC in Britain).

Multi-period: monument built in stages over a long period.

Neolithic: the new stone age, farming societies without the use of metal.

Oligarchy: government by the few.

Passage grave: megalithic chamber, round or polygonal, entered by a passage which is narrower and lower than the chamber; usually covered by a round mound.

Polygonal: many-sided.

Radiocarbon dating: dating based on the measurement of the rate of radioactive decay of carbon-14, found in all living matter. Discovered by Libby in the 1940s, subsequently shown to give answers which were too young, so now calibrated against a timescale derived from tree-ring dating – hence 'cal BC' means a calibrated carbon-14 date.

Stratigraphy: study of superimposed layers, natural or artificial; provides relative dating of events or finds.

Terminal chamber: chamber set at the end of a mound.

Theocracy: government by priests or religious law.

Tholoi: Greek burial chambers similar to western passage graves but now known to be later in date.

Transepted chamber: chamber of complex design with side chambers.

Typological development: a sequence of development derived from the study of changes in shape or style of buildings or artefacts.

10
Sites to visit

Abbreviations

Ant J	Antiquaries Journal
Arch	Archaeologia
Arch Camb	Archaeologia Cambrensis
BA	bronze age
ch	chamber
Corn Arch	Cornish Archaeology
CS	Cotswold-Severn cairn
Brecs	Breconshire type
lat	laterally chambered
simple	simple terminal chamber
trans	transepted chamber
DAJ	Derbyshire Archaeological Journal
dec	decorated
EG	entrance grave
LB	long barrow
LC	long cairn

ME	mortuary enclosure
PD	portal dolmen
PG	passage grave
PPS	Proceedings of the Prehistoric Society
PSAS	Proceedings of the Society of Antiquaries of Scotland
RB	round barrow (bronze age)
RM	round mound (neolithic)
sq	square
SB	stone box chamber
TDGNHAS	Transactions of the Dumfries and Galloway Natural History and Antiquarian Society

* denotes a site in public ownership (English Heritage, Cadw, Historic Scotland or National Trust)

ENGLAND

BERKSHIRE
Inkpen Long Barrow (SU 365623): well-sited LB with ditches.

BUCKINGHAMSHIRE
Whiteleaf Barrow (SP 822040): RM (*PPS* 20, 1954, 212-30).

CORNWALL
Brane (SW 402282): EG.
Lanyon Quoit* (SW 430336): rebuilt chamber.
Pennance (SW 447376): EG.
Tregiffian, St Buryan (SW 430244): EG.
Trethevy Quoit* (SX 259688): spectacular PD.
Zennor Quoit (SW 469380): PD.

DERBYSHIRE
Five Wells (SK 124710): two chambers back to back.
Green Low (SK 232580): ch and broad passage (*DAJ* 85, 1965, 1-24).
Minninglow (SK 209573): three chambers (*DAJ* 102, 1982, 8-22).

DORSET
Pimperne Long Barrow (ST 917105): fine LB with ditches.
Thickthorn Long Barrows (ST 971123): two ditched LBs (*PPS* 2, 1936, 77-96)

GLOUCESTERSHIRE
Belas Knap* (SP 021254): CS lat.

Hetty Pegler's Tump* (SO 789000): CS trans.
Notgrove* (SP 095212): CS trans (*Arch* 86, 1936, 119-62).
Nympsfield (SO 794013): CS trans (*PPS* 45, 1979, 53-91).
Randwick* (SO 825069): CS simple.

HAMPSHIRE
Giant's Grave Long Barrow, Whitsbury (SU 139200): 3 metres high LB.
Gran's Barrow, Rockbourne, and **Knap Barrow** (SU 090198 and 089199): two LBs only 183 metres apart.
Lamborough Long Barrow (SU 593284): impressive LB near road.

HEREFORDSHIRE
Arthur's Stone, Dorstone* (SO 318431): CS Brecs.

ISLES OF SCILLY
Bant's Cairn, St Mary's* (SV 911123): EG (*Corn Arch* 15, 1976, 11-26).
Porth Hellick Down, St Mary's* (SV 928108): EG.

KENT
Coldrum* (TQ 654607): stone chamber at end of long mound.
Kit's Coty House* (TQ 745608): stone chamber at end of long mound.

LINCOLNSHIRE
Deadmen's Graves, Claxby (TF 445719): two LBs.
Giants' Hills, Skendleby (TF 428711): LB (*Arch* 85, 1936, 37-106).

OXFORDSHIRE
Wayland's Smithy* (SU 281854): two periods – CS trans and LB (*PPS* 57, 1991, 61-101).

SOMERSET
Stoney Littleton* (ST 735572): restored CS trans.

WILTSHIRE
Giant's Grave, Milton Lilbourne (SU 198583): LB.
Lugbury Cairn (ST 831786): CS with false portal.
Tilshead White Barrow* (SU 033468): LB, predates BA boundary.
West Kennet 'Long Barrow'* (SU 104677): CS trans (Piggott 1962).
Winterbourne Stoke Long Barrow* (SU 101417): LB with later RBs.

YORKSHIRE, EAST
Willie Howe (TA 063724): huge RM.

YORKSHIRE, NORTH
Duggleby Howe (SE 881669): huge RM.
Kepwick Moor (SE 492904): LB.
Scamridge (SE 892861): LB in area of later dykes.
Westow (SE 759652): LB.
Willerby Wold Long Barrow (TA 029761): LB (*PPS* 29, 1963, 173-204).

ISLE OF MAN
Ballafayle* (SC 476901): cairn with LB features.

Cashtel yn Ard* (SC 463893): Clyde ch + façade (*Ant J* 16, 1936, 373-95).
King Orry's Grave* (SC 440844): dual-chambered cairn.

SCOTLAND

BORDERS (Berwickshire and Roxburghshire)
Long Knowe (NY 527862): LC.
Mutiny Stones (NT 622590): LC (90 metres).

DUMFRIES AND GALLOWAY (Kirkcudbrightshire and Wigtownshire)
Cairnholy I and II* (NX 517358): two multi-period cairns (*PSAS* 83, 1948-9, 103-61).
Mid Gleniron I and II (NX 188610): two multi-period cairns with simple ch (*TDGNHAS* 46, 1969, 29-90).
Slewcairn (NX 924614): hybrid wood and stone monument.
White Cairn, Bargrennan (NX 352783): rectangular PG (*PSAS* 83, 1948-9, 103-61).

FIFE
Balfarg* (NO 281031): reconstructed wood ME (*PSAS* 123, 1993, 43-210).

GRAMPIAN (Banff and Kincardine)
Cairn Catto (NK 074421): LC.
Capo (NO 633664): LC in forest (signposted).
Longman Hill (NJ 737620): LC, possibly two-period.

HIGHLAND (Caithness, Inverness-shire, Skye)
Camster* (ND 260440): two cairns, long, short, with forecourts.
Clava Cairns* (NH 752439-760445): late PGs + stone circles.
Corrimony* (NH 383303): Clava cairn + circle (*PSAS* 88, 1954-6, 171-207).
Rudh' an Dunain, Skye (NG 393163): PG + façade (*PSAS* 66, 1931-2, 183-99).
Tulach an t'Sionnaich (ND 070619): complex PG/LC (*PSAS* 98, 1965-6, 1-75).

ORKNEY
Blackhammer, Rousay* (HY 414276): stalled PG in LC.
Cuween Hill, Mainland* (HY 363127): PG + four side chambers.
Isbister, South Ronaldsay (ND 470846): stalled PG + side cells (Hedges 1987).
Knowe of Yarso, Rousay* (HY 404279): stalled PG in LC.
Maes Howe, Mainland* (HY 318127): magnificent cruciform PG.
Midhowe, Rousay* (HY 372304): immense stalled PG in LC.
Quoyness, Sanday* (HY 676378): PG + six side chambers.
Taversoe Tuick, Rousay* (HY 425276): unusual two-storey PG.
Unstan, Mainland* (HY 282117): stalled PG + side cell.
Wideford Hill, Mainland* (HY 409121): PG + three large side chambers.

SHETLAND
Pund's Water (HU 324712): heel-shaped cairn.

STRATHCLYDE (Argyll and Arran)
Achnacreebeag (NM 929364): SB + simple PG (*PSAS* 102, 1969-70, 31-55).
Beacharra (NR 692433): Clyde cairn (*PPS* 30, 1964, 134-58).
Brackley (NR 794418): Clyde cairn (*PSAS* 89, 1955-6, 22-54).
Carn Ban, Arran* (NR 990262): Clyde cairn + façade.
Crarae House (NR 987974): Clyde cairn (*PSAS* 94, 1960-1, 1-27).
Loch Nell South, Dalineun (NM 880266): SB.

Nether Largie South* (NR 828978): Clyde cairn.
Torrylin, Arran* (NR 955210): Clyde cairn + portals.

WESTERN ISLES
Barpa Langass, North Uist (NF 838657): simple PG.
Callanish, Lewis* (NB 213330): PG in stone circle.
Clettraval, North Uist (NF 749713): odd Clyde cairn (also iron age wheelhouse) (*PSAS* 69, 1934-5, 480-536).
Unival, North Uist (NF 800668): simple PG, sq cairn (*PSAS* 82, 1947-8, 1-49).

WALES
ANGLESEY
Barclodiad y Gawres* (SH 329707): dec cruciform PG (Daniel and Powell 1956).
Bodowyr* (SH 463682): simple PG.
Bryn Celli Ddu* (SH 507702): late PG overlying henge (*Arch* 80, 1930, 179-214; Lynch 1991, 91-101).
Din Dryfol* (SH 395724): rectangular ch (Smith & Lynch 1987).
Lligwy* (SH 501860): huge capstone over sunken chamber.
Presaddfed* (SH 347809): two ch, possibly multi-period.
Trefignath* (SH 259805): multi-period three ch (Smith and Lynch 1987).
Ty Newydd* (SH 344738): simple PG.

GLAMORGAN
Arthur's Stone, Gower* (SS 491906): impressive capstone.
Parc le Breos Cwm, Gower* (SS 537898): CS trans.
St Lythans* (ST 100722): CS simple.
Tinkinswood* (ST 092733): CS simple (*Arch Camb* 1915, 253-320; 1916, 239-67).

GWENT
Garn Lwyd (ST 447968): CS chamber (lat?).

GWYNEDD (Caernarfonshire and Merioneth)
Bachwen (SH 407495): rectangular ch with cupmarks on capstone.
Capel Garmon* (SH 818543): CS Brecs (*Arch Camb* 1927, 1-44).
Carneddau Hengwm (SH 613205): two cairns: PD and CS lat.
Dyffryn Ardudwy* (SH 588228): two-period PD (*Arch* 104, 1973, 1-49).
Lletty'r Filiast, Great Orme (SH 772829): rectangular ch.
Maen y Bardd (SH 740717): rectangular ch, probably PD.
Tan y Muriau (SH 238288): PD in multi-period(?) cairn.

PEMBROKESHIRE
Carreg Coetan Arthur, Newport* (SN 060393): PD.
Carreg Samson (SM 848335): simple PG (*Arch Camb* 124, 1975, 15-35).
Coetan Arthur, St David's (SM 725280): ruined ch on fine headland.
Hanging Stone, Rosemarket (SM 972082): simple PG.
Pentre Ifan* (SN 099370): PD + façade (*Arch Camb* 100, 1949, 3-23; Lynch 1972).

POWYS (Breconshire)
Gwernvale (SO 211192): CS Brecs (Britnell and Savory 1984).
Little Lodge (SO 182380): CS Brecs.
Pen y Wyrlod I, Llanigon (SO 225398) CS Brecs.

11
Further reading

General studies

Ashbee, P. *The Earthen Long Barrow in Britain.* Geo Books, Norwich, second edition 1984.

Chapman, R.W., *et al* (editors). *The Archaeology of Death.* Cambridge University Press, Cambridge, 1981.

Corcoran, J.X.W.P. 'Multi-period Construction and the Origins of the Chambered Long Cairn in Western Britain and Ireland' in F. Lynch and C. Burgess (editors), *Prehistoric Man in Wales and the West*, 31-63. Adams & Dart, Bath, 1972.

Daniel, G.E. *The Prehistoric Chambered Tombs of England and Wales.* Cambridge University Press, Cambridge, 1950.

Daniel, G.E., and Kjaerum, P. (editors). *Megalithic Graves and Ritual.* Jutland Archaeological Society, Aarhus,1973.

Darvill, T. *The Megalithic Chambered Tombs of the Cotswold-Severn Region.* Vorda, Highworth, 1982.

Darvill, T. *Prehistoric Britain.* Batsford, London, 1987.

Dyer, J. (editor). *Discovering Prehistoric England.* Shire, Princes Risborough, 1993.

Evans, J.D., *et al* (editors). *Antiquity and Man: Essays in Honour of Glyn Daniel.* Thames & Hudson, 1981. Part II separately reprinted in 1983 as *The Megalithic Monuments of Western Europe* (editor C. Renfrew).

Greenwell, W. *British Barrows.* Clarendon Press, Oxford, 1877.

Henshall, A.S. *Chambered Tombs in Scotland* (two volumes). Edinburgh University Press, Edinburgh, 1963 and 1972.

Joussaume, R. *Dolmens for the Dead: Megalith Building Throughout the World.* Batsford, London, 1988.

Kinnes, I. 'Monumental Function in British Neolithic Burial Practices', *World Archaeology* 7, 1975, 16-29.

Kinnes, I. *Round Barrows and Ring-Ditches in the British Neolithic.* British Museum, London, 1979.

Kinnes, I. *Non-Megalithic Long Barrows and Allied Structures in the British Neolithic.* British Museum, London, 1992.

Lynch, F.M. 'Towards a Chronology of Megalithic Tombs in Wales' in G.C. Boon and J.M. Lewis (editors), *Welsh Antiquity: Essays Presented to H.N. Savory*, 63-79. National Museum of Wales, Cardiff, 1976.

Lynch, F.M. *Prehistoric Anglesey.* Anglesey Antiquarian Society, Llangefni, second edition 1991.

Manby, T. 'Long Barrows of Northern England', *Scottish Archaeological Forum* 2, 1970, 1-28.

Megaw, J.V.S, and Simpson, D.D.A. *Introduction to British Prehistory.* Leicester University Press, Leicester, 1979.

Mohen, J-P. *The World of Megaliths.* Facts on File, New York, 1990.

Mortimer, J.R. *Forty Years Researches in the British and Saxon Burial Mounds of East Yorkshire.* A. Brown & Sons, London, 1905.

Parker Pearson, M. *Bronze Age Britain.* English Heritage, London, 1993.

Powell, T.G.E., *et al. Megalithic Enquiries in the West of Britain.* Liverpool University Press, Liverpool, 1969.

Renfrew, A.C. (editor). *British Prehistory: A New Outline.* London, 1974.

Renfrew, A.C. *Investigations in Orkney.* Society of Antiquaries, London, 1979.

Sharples, N., and Sheridan, A. (editors). *Vessels for the Ancestors: Essays on the Neolithic of Britain and Ireland in Honour of Audrey Henshall.* Edinburgh University Press, Edinburgh, 1992.

Shee Twohig, E. *Irish Megalithic Tombs.* Shire, Princes Risborough, 1990.

Sherratt, A. 'The Genesis of Megaliths: Monumentality, Ethnicity and Social Complexity in Neolithic North-west Europe', *World Archaeology* 22, 1990, 147-67.

Startin, W., and Bradley, R. 'Some Notes on Work Organisation and Society in Prehistoric Wessex' in C. Ruggles and A. Whittle (editors), *Astronomy and Society in Britain During the Period 4000-1500 BC,* 289-96. British Archaeological Reports, Oxford, 1981.

Excavation reports
(See also chapter 10, 'Sites to Visit'.)

Ashbee, P. 'The Fussell's Lodge Long Barrow Excavations, 1957', *Archaeologia* 100, 1966, 1-80.

Ashbee, P., *et al.* 'Excavation of Three Long Barrows near Avebury, Wiltshire', *Proceedings of the Prehistoric Society* 45, 1979, 207-300.

Britnell, W.J., and Savory, H.N. *Gwernvale and Penywyrlod: Two Neolithic Long Cairns in the Black Mountains of Brecknock.* Cambrian Archaeological Monographs 2, Cardiff, 1984.

Coombs, D. 'Callis Wold Round Barrow, Humberside', *Antiquity* 50, 1976, 130-1.

Daniel, G.E., and Powell, T.G.E. *Barclodiad y Gawres: the Excavation of a Megalithic Chambered Tomb in Anglesey.* Liverpool University Press, Liverpool, 1956.

Drewett, P. 'The Excavation of an Oval Burial Mound of the Third

Millennium BC at Alfriston, East Sussex, 1974', *Proceedings of the Prehistoric Society* 41, 1975, 119-52.

Hedges, J. *Tomb of the Eagles*. Murray, London, 1987.

Henshall, A.S. 'Manx Megaliths Again: an Attempt at Structural Analysis' in P. Davey (editor), *Man and Environment in the Isle of Man*. British Archaeological Reports, Oxford, 1978.

Holgate, R. 'The Medway Megaliths and Neolithic Kent', *Archaeologia Cantiana* 97, 1981, 221-34.

Jackson, D.A. 'The Excavation of Neolithic and Bronze Age Sites at Aldwincle, Northants, 1967-71', *Northamptonshire Archaeology* 11, 1976, 12-70.

Keiller, A., and Piggott, S. 'Excavation of an Untouched Chamber in the Lanhill Long Barrow', *Proceedings of the Prehistoric Society* 4, 1938, 122-50.

Lynch, F.M. 'Portal Dolmens in the Nevern Valley, Pembrokeshire' in F. Lynch and C. Burgess (editors), *Prehistoric Man in Wales and the West*, 67-84. Adams & Dart, Bath, 1972.

MacKie, E.W. 'New Excavations on the Monamore Neolithic Chambered Cairn, Lamlash, Isle of Arran, in 1961', *Proceedings of the Society of Antiquaries of Scotland* 97, 1963-4, 1-34.

Manby, T. 'The Excavation of the Kilham Long Barrow, East Riding of Yorkshire', *Proceedings of the Prehistoric Society* 42, 1976, 111-60.

Masters, L. 'The Lochhill Long Cairn', *Antiquity* 47, 1973, 96-100.

Morgan, F. de M. 'The Excavation of a Long Barrow at Nutbane, Hampshire', *Proceedings of the Prehistoric Society* 25, 1959, 15-51.

Piggott, S. *The West Kennet Long Barrow: Excavations 1955-6*. HMSO, London, 1962.

Piggott, S. 'Excavation of the Dalladies Long Barrow, Fettercairn, Kincardineshire', *Proceedings of the Society of Antiquaries of Scotland* 104, 1971-2, 23-47.

Saville, A. *Hazleton North: the Excavation of a Neolithic Long Cairn of the Cotswold-Severn Group*. English Heritage, London, 1990.

Shand, P., and Hodder, I. 'Haddenham', *Current Archaeology* 118, 1990, 339-44.

Smith, C.A., and Lynch, F.M. *Trefignath and Din Dryfol: the Excavation of Two Megalithic Tombs in Anglesey*. Cambrian Archaeological Monographs 3, Cardiff, 1987.

Vatcher, F. de M. 'The Excavation of the Long Mortuary Enclosure on Normanton Down, Wiltshire', *Proceedings of the Prehistoric Society* 26, 1961, 160-73.

Vyner, B. 'The Excavation of a Neolithic Cairn at Street House, Loftus, Cleveland', *Proceedings of the Prehistoric Society* 50, 1984, 151-95.

Index

Page numbers in italic refer to illustrations